BABY FACE

BABY FACE

CELEBRATING YOUR PREGNANCY AND BABY WITH BEAUTIFUL PHOTO CRAFTS

BARBARA SMITH

Foreword by Graham Nash

Watson-Guptill Publications/New York

To Ken, who knew I could.

First published in 2008 by Watson-Guptill Publications,
Nielsen Business Media, a division of The Nielsen Company
770 Broadway, New York, NY 10003
www.watsonguptill.com

Library of Congress Cataloging-in-Publication Data

Smith, Barbara.
 Baby face : celebrating your pregnancy and baby with beautiful photo crafts / Barbara Smith.
    p. cm.
 Includes index.
 ISBN-13: 978-0-8174-4116-6 (alk. paper)
 ISBN-10: 0-8174-4116-6 (alk. paper)
 1. Photograph albums. 2. Scrapbooks. 3. Pregnancy. 4. Childbirth. I. Title.
 TR465.S655 2008
 745.593--dc22
            2007029100

Editorial Director: Victoria Craven
Senior Acquisitions Editor: Abigail Wilentz
Senior Development Editor: Michelle Bredeson
Designer: 3+Co.
Senior Production Manager: Salvatore Destro

Manufactured in China

First printing, 2008

1 2 3 4 5 6 7 8 9 / 16 15 14 13 12 11 10 09 08

When using cutting tools and other suggested products, readers are strongly cautioned to follow manufacturers' directions, to heed warnings, and to seek prompt medical attention for an injury. In addition, readers are advised to keep all potentially harmful supplies away from children.

Acknowledgments

Since this book is, in essence, about family, I'd like to take this opportunity to thank *my* own family, and my family of friends, for their love and support in every which way: my amazing mother, Evelyn Schultz; my sweet, adorable, and ever helpful brothers, Keith and Kevin Schultz; my dear sister, Terry Brodbeck; my fabulous daughter, Erin, her wonderful husband, Brian, and my precious Leila and Hana Kalliel; best friends for life Judy and Ken Ravitz, Joani Stewart, Susan and Graham Nash, Alex Sandlin, Jerry Freedman, and Paul Joseph. And Kim, just because.

My heartfelt thanks go to those who allowed me to share and photograph some of their most precious moments: Suzy Skaar and Annika; Danielle Edell; Nicole and Scott Lear; Janelle Hensley; Staci, Scott, and Stella Koondel; Caterina Gennaro and Taylor and Austin Kurr; Alison and Michael Lotterstein; Susan, Brian, and Ian Sullivan; Luciana Topping; Kim and Jimmy Higgins; Rosanna and Kerry O'Brien; Amanda and Carl Mueller; Jimmi, Jasmine, and Logan Johnson; Ariana Lambert Smeraldo; Indigo Ponzone-Garamella, Tiffany, David, and Raylynn Sampson; the Sandoz family; and the Swedelson family.

I'm profoundly grateful for the exceptionally fine products and professional support of Epson (Dan Steinberg), Tamron (Stacie Errera), and Crane & Co. (David Williams). Skip Cohen (Rangefinder Publishing, Inc.) continues to provide support and encouragement, and in the process has become a trusted and true friend. And, finally, to Michelle Bredeson at Watson-Guptill, my special thanks for another enjoyable experience. You're the best!

Contents

Foreword

"Our house is a very, very, very fine house
With two cats in the yard
Life used to be so hard
Now everything is easy 'cos of you"

Anyone who knows me knows that "home" is where my heart is, and I truly believe that my family is the most important element of my life. My wife and children have often found themselves in focus (or deliberately out of focus) before my lens. A longtime family friend, Barbara has been witness to the evocative shots I took of my wife, Susan, when she was pregnant, and of each of our three children over almost thirty years. One of my favorites is a photo I took of my first son, Jackson, when he was about five years old. In it, he always reminds me of a child looking at this fragile world and wondering. It's so strange that an image I took makes me feel so humble.

In turn, I have been witness to Barbara's amazing metamorphosis from, believe it or not, court stenographer to artist. I remember the many times she would come to our house and immediately gravitate to whatever photographs happened to be within her line of vision (some Edward S. Curtis orotones come to mind), asking questions, always eager to learn more. Like most artists, she started off innocently enough, not realizing that, in time, her passion would overcome practicality and art would become her life. That passion comes shining through in this book, and I'm proud to have been somewhat instrumental in inspiring her. I'm quite sure she will inspire you in turn. As my friend Paul Simon once said, "Preserve your memories; they're all that's left you."

Graham Nash
2008

In the projects in this book, you'll combine imagery and paper arts to share the stories inherent in your best photos.

Introduction

For over thirty years, pregnancy, babies, photography, and custom stationery have been constants in my life, lovingly intertwined. You might say I was ahead of my time. While pregnant with my daughter in 1972—long before a visibly pregnant Demi Moore graced the cover of *Vanity Fair*—I asked a photographer friend to shoot me and my long-haired sweetie in the nude (us, not him!) and turned my favorite shot into a holiday card. On the cover, it read "We're expecting," and then on the inside, "you to have a Merry Christmas and a Happy New Year!" Kind of corny, but definitely unique. Decades later, I shot pregnancy portraits of my daughter, and I was there in the delivery room snapping away when each of her children was born. I made shower invitations, thank-you notes, birth announcements, and baby albums for each of these special occasions. So while I have become a professional in the field today, my passion really stems from being a nonprofessional—an expectant and then new parent, and a member of a growing family.

With both digital photography and scrapbooking having become so immensely popular, people are taking more and more family photos, and they're getting better at it. My bet is that you've taken lots of pictures that are as good as if not better than many of mine. But I do have a few things to share that you may not know about, and it is in that spirit that I reach out to you.

In this book, you'll find lots of helpful shooting tips as well as stimulating ideas for bringing new life to your favorite images. You'll learn how to combine both art and craft to produce useful, beautiful, and evocative pieces of stationery, gifts, and albums destined to enjoy an afterlife as cherished keepsakes. But this is only a reference guide—your creative interpretation is key.

One of the most exciting and enjoyable aspects of this endeavor is the ability to combine the old with the new, traditional with contemporary, and handcrafted with machine-made in countless unique, satisfying, and effective designs. We can choose from watercolor papers, specialty papers, and digital printing papers; images shot with film or with digital cameras; traditional or digital fine art techniques and alternative processes; black-and-white, toned, or color photographs; embellishments such as ribbons or dried flowers; art supply store findings or found objects; and an ever-expanding world of typefaces.

Technology now enables us to send images over our cell phones and via e-mail quickly and easily. These are often ideal methods for sending a message and a snapshot to someone. But by combining meaningful photographs with papercrafts and then snail-mailing or hand delivering them, we add the warmth of the personal touch. The underlying message in sending a handcrafted item is, "You're special."

So, starting today, I hope you will begin using your favorite photos to create unique announcements, invitations, holiday cards, and more. You can even make simple books commemorating special events—birthdays, outings, vacations—or even a typical day in the life of your family. Nothing makes a more meaningful gift for a loved one or a more treasured keepsake!

CHAPTER 1

Papercrafting Basics

Papercrafting is, first and foremost, FUN! It's something almost anyone can do, because there are no difficult skills to learn. Indeed, papercrafting appeals to the child in each of us who just loves to cut and paste or make paper dolls or airplanes. Now we're going to expand on those basics—cutting, pasting, and folding—finessing them through the use of the proper materials, tools, and techniques.

A Paper Primer

The paper you select as the foundation for each piece of stationery you create plays an important role in its overall design—it can actually make or break the effect you wish to achieve. You'll find a wonderful selection of diverse papers in art supply, office supply, scrapbooking, and stationery stores, as well as online. Each paper's texture, weight, and thickness will determine its use. For instance, you may want to use a heavier decorative paper for the cover of a card or note, then line it with a lighter weight paper on which the text is printed. Unless you're adhering your printed layout to a decorative backing or using it as a liner or insert, choose printing paper with strong character.

Paper is a versatile and exciting medium for creative self-expression, and each type of paper has a distinctive personality—you might even say a will of its own. For instance, most paper has a *grain*, the direction in which the fibers lie. Paper resists being torn or folded against its grain, so find the grain and plan your layout accordingly. That being said, if you happen to have a piece of stock of a certain size that necessitates folding or cutting against the grain, go ahead and inflict your will upon it. The piece simply may not fold quite as neatly or lie as flat as it would otherwise.

This Valentine's card combines six different papers. The foundation is heavyweight card stock to which two types of handmade papers are adhered. The photo is printed on inkjet photo paper, the text is printed on a sheet of copier paper, and the flower is made out of mulberry paper.

Going with the Grain

These simple exercises illustrate the concept of grain: Take a sheet of newspaper and tear it in different directions. Notice how easily it tears in one direction—along the grain—but not in the other. With heavier paper or card stock (stiff, thick, or sturdy paper or cardboard), hold a sheet by opposite edges and gently move them toward each other, taking note of the degree of resistance. Now rotate the sheet a quarter turn and do the same. The card has more "give" when bent along the grain.

Printing Papers

Available at computer and office supply stores and through the Internet, papers created specifically for your printer, be it laser, inkjet, or something else, will yield the best results as far as clarity and tone. Before buying a particular paper, check the specifications to see if it is compatible with the printer you will be using. Your printer can likely accept a wide variety of paper thicknesses, including card stock and envelopes.

For double-sided printing, be sure to use printing paper designated as such. Printing on the "wrong" side is certain to produce a substandard result and may actually harm your printer.

Don't try to print on paper that has loose components (such as fibers or flower petals) that could catch or fall off into the printer and cause serious damage. Textured paper tends to absorb more ink that can then bleed, making your image or text appear soft and even difficult to read. The following papers are ideally suited for imprinting both text and imagery.

ARCHES INFINITY

Arches Infinity Museum Quality Digital Art and Photo Inkjet Paper produces beautiful results. Arches Infinity Smooth Natural White is a high-quality fine art paper with a creamy, warm color and a velvety texture, offered in two weights. Arches Infinity is also available in a pebbly textured surface in two weights.

CRANE

Synonymous with fine paper for over two hundred years, Crane has joined the digital revolution, producing several truly outstanding products. Museo II is a 100-percent cotton rag digital fine art paper with two printable sides. Finally, a heavyweight card stock that is perfect for elegant invitations as well as postcards! It's the paper I turn to most often these days!

EPSON

Epson inkjet printers are arguably the state-of-the-art for digital printing, and Epson's line of digital papers is not only dependable but versatile. Epson papers include Presentation Paper Matte, Double-Sided Matte Paper, Premium Glossy Photo Paper, Premium Luster Photo Paper, and Velvet Fine Art Paper.

HAHNEMÜHLE

Somewhere within its three Lumijet collections—Portfolio Series, Preservation Series, and Inkjet Fine Art Papers—you'll find the perfect medium for just about any project, including dual-sided, parchment, woven, and "canvas" papers.

HAWK MOUNTAIN PAPERS

A friendly, family-owned business, Hawk Mountain has a wide assortment of American-made digital papers for just about every purpose, and at very reasonable prices.

SOMERSET

Somerset Velvet Photo Enhanced is another excellent fine art paper, which is moldmade in England. Be aware that once you've removed the paper from the package, it's almost impossible to differentiate one side from the other, yet it's critical to print on the correct side.

Digital printing papers are coated to make them suitable for imprinting both text and imagery, although some are better suited to photographic reproduction than others. Several brands have an appealing fine art quality—a tactile surface with a weight befitting a significant occasion or a cherished photo.

Crane's Museo II paper is available in two weights, and in precut and prescored "Artist Cards" with coordinating envelopes.

Decorative Papers

Most art supply stores sell decorative and watercolor papers in letter size as well as "parent" sheets—usually about 22 x 30 inches—that can be cut down to size as needed. Store paper in a dry place and keep it flat, if possible, or loosely rolled. These types of papers are not coated for printing and are best used as foundations, album pages, or as decorative elements.

WATERCOLOR PAPERS

Most watercolor paper is made from 100-percent cotton rag, has a neutral pH value that makes it acid free, has deckled edges, and is watermarked. It's usually available in three weights—90 pound, 140 pound, and 300 pound—and in three textures—hot pressed (smooth), cold pressed (medium texture), and rough (the most texture). Including the beautiful deckled edge of a piece of watercolor paper adds a special touch to a card or album.

SPECIALTY PAPERS

There are many beautiful handmade, mold-made, or machine-made specialty papers available. From far and near—Japan, Egypt, India, Thailand, Taiwan, the Philippines, and the United States—these unusual and often exquisite papers can be expensive, but they add a decidedly handcrafted quality to cards and albums. You'll find many colors and textures to choose from. These papers often do not have a grain.

Gorgeous handmade, moldmade, and machine-made specialty papers in myriad colors and textures are available from around the world.

CANSON MI-TEINTES

Canson Mi-Teintes is an easy-to-find paper with a textured surface. It's available in a veritable rainbow of solid colors.

VELLUM

Most suitable as an overlay with or without text, translucent vellum adds visual interest to stationery items by imparting a soft, appealing look to the photo or text lying beneath. There's an array of colors to choose from, as well as patterned, embossed, and even metallic finishes. A few types of vellum are suitable for inkjet printing, but the ink will pool on the surface of most. When in doubt, experiment first, and always let each sheet dry undisturbed.

Sometimes the materials themselves can suggest a theme. Here the pearlescent quality of both the paper and ribbon inspired the message. Details of the newborn and a photo are printed on an inside liner sheet. (Font: Zapfino)

THEMED AND PATTERNED PAPERS

Explore the scrapbooking section of craft stores for other types of specialty papers you can incorporate into your stationery.

CARD STOCK

Also known as cover paper, card stock is a stiff, rigid paper that is commonly used for post-cards, greeting cards, and soft book covers.

Archival Considerations

In making special stationery and other keepsakes, we want to create mementos to be cherished for years to come. Whenever possible, use products—especially paper and adhesives—bearing the words "acid free" or "archival." Acid-free products have a pH value of 7.0 or higher and resist deterioration. Many of the products listed here are archival, but some are not.

The Toolbox

Sure, you can get by with school-grade plastic rulers, chewed-up pencils, dull scissors, and humble paste, but you need only a few tools to get started on the projects in this book, so why not invest in quality, then add to your toolbox as you gain experience and enthusiasm for the craft.

Cutting tools include a knife, corner rounder, scissors, decorative scissors, hole punch, and paper cutter.

An Ellison die cutter is worth its considerable weight—47 pounds—in gold for cutting windows in book and album covers. Custom dies can be made to your specifications.

Cutting Tools

Using the correct tool for the job at hand will make your life oh-so-much easier.

- **Paper cutter**—for making straight cuts
- **Craft or utility knife with replaceable blade**—for straight cuts and for cutting windows
- **Die cutter**—a piece of rather heavy equipment for one-step cutting of windows and shapes; great for repetitive work, especially if you plan to devote a lot of time and energy to papercrafting
- **Sharp scissors**—a small pair for detail work such as trimming photos and cutting out other paper designs and shapes
- **Decorative scissors**—for creating special edges such as ripples, zigzags, and scallops
- **Hole punch**—for making holes for eyelets or for threading ribbon or fiber
- **Corner rounder**—a paper punch for rounding off sharp corners

Adhesives

There are several types of adhesives available for different aspects of papercrafting, and several brands within each category. You'll come to prefer one over another as time goes by. My workstation contains the following adhesives.

GLUE

- **Acid-free glue sticks**—for adhering small, irregular-shaped surfaces and for mounting small background sheets to pages
- **Lineco Neutral pH Adhesive**— for papercrafting, collage, and bookbinding
- **Yes! Paste**—acid free and won't curl or wrinkle paper, no matter how lightweight it is; can be thinned with warm distilled water, is transparent when applied, and dries quickly
- **Scotch Quick Dry Tacky Adhesive**—its small applicator tip makes it perfect for applying glue to edges

TAPE

- **Double-sided tape**—Scotch/3M makes an acid-free photo and document tape that is neater and easier to use than glue
- **Drafting or removable tape**—can be used to hold items in place temporarily or while positioning them
- **Linen hinging tape**—for attaching a mat to a backing board; Lineco manufactures a self-adhesive archival product that makes the hinging process quick and easy

PHOTO CORNERS OR CORNER MOUNTS

These hold photos securely but also allow easy removal, if needed. The corners are affixed to the page and the photo is slipped in. They are available in a variety of colors and designs. The self-adhesive corners are easier to use than the type that must be moistened first. Lineco makes clear self-adhesive archival corners that can be used when you don't want them to show.

PHOTO SPLITS OR MOUNTING TABS

These double-sided self-adhesive stickers are used for mounting photos or other papers.

SPRAY ADHESIVE

This product produces a fine, sticky mist that is efficient for adhering large surfaces. Some types allow repositioning; others do not.

Sticky stuff, including archival linen hinging tape, photo corners, temporary and double-sided tape, and several kinds of glue.

TIP

To retain spray (and/or to protect the surrounding area from overspray), make a spray booth from a large cardboard box. Before each use, lay down a clean liner of newspaper to prevent items—especially photographs—from sticking or picking up residue from prior applications. Always spray outdoors or in a well-ventilated area to avoid inhaling harmful vapors.

Miscellaneous Tools

These additional items will make your job easier and help give your work a professional, polished finish:

- Ruler—metal with cork bottoms are best; the metal is durable and doesn't get nicked by craft knives, and the cork bottom prevents slippage
- "Self-healing" cutting mats—protect work surfaces and extend the life of craft knife blades; they also have grids that make measuring a breeze
- Bone folder—a flat tool used to create clean, crisp folds, to score, and to burnish
- Pencil and eraser—for marking and erasing layouts
- Marvy/Uchida Liquid Gold opaque paint marker—use the broad-line tip for gilding the edges of card stock; for lettering, use the extra fine point
- Light box—helpful for lining up design elements and for lettering
- Punch set and rubber mallet—for making spine holes in handmade books

More Fun Tools

Here are some handy, although not essential, gadgets that are available at most hobby and scrapbook shops:

- Paper punches—to add small design motifs such as a fleur-de-lis; corner rounders are also available
- Paper crimper—gives paper (and other materials such as foil) a "corrugated" or rippled texture
- Calligraphy pens and markers—for hand lettering
- Glue gun—for adhering millinery and other three-dimensional objects
- Eyelets and eyelet setter, brads, metal alphabets—fun stuff!

Some useful supplies to have on hand include a self-healing cutting mat, bone folder, pencil with eraser, metallic markers, calligraphy pens, ruler, circle cutter, eyelet setter, punch set, and glue gun.

Basic Techniques

The papercrafting techniques required for the projects in this book are simple—mostly folding and cutting—but doing them well requires practice. And do them well we must, because we're creating keepsakes of some of life's most special occasions.

Folding

When using heavy paper or card stock, always score the paper first for a crisp, clean fold: Use a ruler or straightedge in conjunction with the grid on a self-healing cutting mat to determine where the fold belongs. Place the ruler or straightedge in position and run the pointed end of a bone folder along the edge, creating an indentation or groove in the paper. For especially thick card stock, use a craft knife instead, being careful to penetrate the surface only slightly.

Fold the paper (with the groove on the outside), then burnish with the long edge of the bone folder to sharpen the crease. To prevent the paper from becoming shiny, lay a piece of scrap paper over the fold before burnishing.

Scoring the paper before folding.

Cutting

Using a well-designed paper cutter is the easiest and fastest way to cut straight edges. Self-sharpening roller, or rotary, cutters are generally more accurate than the handle type

Burnishing the folded paper.

and are capable of trimming to a hair's width. Most cutters have a built-in ruler to aid in measuring.

To cut out windows or shapes, use a craft knife with a fresh blade, a steel ruler (the blade can catch in a soft wood or plastic ruler), and a self-healing cutting mat. There's no need to mark up your papers: For neatness and accuracy, use the grid on the mat to measure and align paper while cutting. Hold the knife just as you would a pen, and cut in a firm downward motion.

A rotary cutter makes it simple to cut clean, straight edges.

Faux Deckling

A deckle is the natural rough edge on a mold-made or handmade sheet of paper before it's been trimmed. Almost any paper that can be cut can also be torn for an interesting deckled look. Tear the paper randomly, or tear against the edge of a straight or decorative ruler for more control.

Gilding

To gild the edges of watercolor paper or fine art digital paper, prime a broad-line Liquid Gold marker so that the tip is infused with paint. Place a ruler on the paper about 1/16 inch away from the edge and run the marker toward you along the margin in a smooth stroke. Repeat if necessary. For more delicate gilding, hold the sheet up with one hand and with the other run the tip or the side of the marker along the sharp outside edge of the paper.

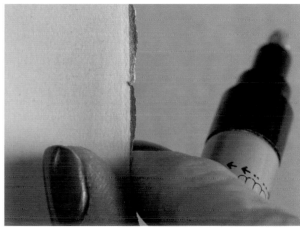

Gilding adds a touch of elegance and luxury.

Hand Lettering

Always practice lettering on a separate piece of paper before attempting to write directly on your card or album page. When writing directly on lightweight paper, vellum, or transparency film, tape a piece of lined paper onto a light box. Turn on the light box, place a blank sheet over it, and write to your heart's content, knowing that your lettering will be perfectly straight. You can also perform this same technique using a window during daylight hours.

TIP

You probably won't want to letter a large number of invitations by hand, but you can certainly create a "camera-ready" master by hand, scan it, import it into Photoshop or other photo-editing program, and output it that way.

Letterpress Printing

Letterpress printing, a technique in which a raised surface is inked and pressed into a sheet of paper, is labor intensive and requires not only a letterpress but a high degree of skill and craftsmanship. Letterpress printing began in Europe in the fifteenth century and eventually gave way to faster and cheaper printing methods, but it has been rediscovered and is one of the biggest trends in stationery. I mention it here because by simply combining appropriate fonts with a heavyweight textured digital paper, you can create a faux letterpress project with similar appeal.

Handmade, Not Homemade

Even if your pieces are being sent to friends and family, you should strive to give them a professional appearance. All edges should be smooth and straight, creases should be sharp, and there should be no telltale signs of glue or tape and absolutely no smudges or wrinkles.

Glossary of Paper-crafting & Fine Art Terms

HERE ARE A FEW TERMS YOU MAY ENCOUNTER WHILE EXPLORING THE JOYS OF PAPERCRAFTING.

- **ARCHIVAL:** Describes paper and other products that have a pH value of 7.0 or higher and resist deterioration.
- **CANVAS:** Can refer literally to canvas textile, or generally to any receptive substrate.
- **COATED PAPER:** Paper with a surface coating that prevents ink from absorbing into the fibers, thereby producing fine detail and rich tones and colors.
- **COLD-PRESSED PAPER:** Roughly textured watercolor paper.
- **COLLAGE:** The layering of materials.
- **DECKLED:** Describes the natural rough edge of a moldmade or handmade sheet of paper.
- **DYE INKS:** Used in some inkjet printers; dye inks have a wider color range than pigment inks but are less permanent.
- **FLOAT MOUNT:** Mounting technique that allows edges of prints to show when framing; to preserve deckled edges when framing, use a float mount instead of a mat.
- **FOUND OBJECTS:** Objects that are not designed for artistic purposes but that may be incorporated into a work of art. Popular items are scraps of paper found on the street, pieces of twisted or rusty metal, or anything that has deteriorated over time and natural items such as seed pods, dried flowers, and feathers.
- **GESSO:** Used to coat a substrate to give it a smooth, absorbent, finely textured ground on which to paint.

- **GRAIN:** The direction in which a paper's fibers lie.
- **HOT-PRESSED PAPER:** Smooth textured watercolor paper.
- **LAZERTRAN:** A "decal" type of transfer paper for use with just about any surface—paper, ceramics, wood, candles, etc. Different versions are available for use with copiers and inkjet printers or for transferring to silk or fabric.
- **MIXED MEDIA:** Describes works of art made with more than one medium, such as photography and paint.
- **PIGMENT INK:** Used in some inkjet printers; has more permanence than dye inks.
- **SUBSTRATE:** A fancy word for "surface."
- **TRANSFER:** Moving an image from one surface to another.
- **WATER SOLUBLE:** Having the ability to dissolve in water.

This birth announcement was printed on heavyweight Arches Infinity Textured paper (355 g/m²). Using dark brown ink contributes to the look of letterpress. (Fonts: Letterpress and P22 Cezanne)

CHAPTER 2

Designing Beautiful Layouts

Most of us respond unconsciously to visual layouts several times a day. Begin paying attention to the printed materials that appear in your life—billboards, magazines, menus. A poorly designed piece will cause you to hesitate before reading it, even to ignore it, whereas a strong layout will draw you in and actually lead you through it. In this chapter, we'll explore ideas and techniques for creating layouts for invitations, cards, and birth announcements that are a pleasure to behold and sure to be cherished.

Graphic Design Basics

....

Graphic design is simply the art of arranging images and text to communicate a message. Sounds like a must for the items we'll be creating, and it is! Although you certainly don't need to be a graphic artist to design strong printed pieces, it helps to understand a few basic principles.

Thanks to Photoshop and its Layers feature, it's incredibly easy to experiment with graphic design digitally. But whether you prefer to work on your computer, on a piece of paper, or by cutting and pasting in a visual journal (see "The Visual Journal" on page 28), start with an idea—a design concept—and then just play. Throw stuff out there, move things around, add things, take things away. Keep what you love, but then refine the piece by considering the following:

- Is there visual interest?
- Will someone want to read this?
- Is the piece clear and well organized?
- Is it accurate?
- Is it simple? Even the most complex ideas, when refined, appear simple. That's what makes us say, "I could have done that!" or "Why didn't I think of that?"
- Is there a sense of balance? There should be plenty of "negative" space—that is, empty space surrounding the various elements—to balance the graphics.
- Does it flow? The eye should move effortlessly from one element to the next.

To accomplish these ends, create unity through the following:

- A strong focal point that immediately catches the eye (e.g., a photograph).
- Proximity or grouping of information that belongs together (e.g., invitation specifics, such as date, time, place).
- Repetition of graphic design elements (e.g., bullets, dingbats, lines, and shapes).
- Alignment of text blocks and other elements along their top, bottom, left, or right edges so that they don't appear haphazardly placed on the page.

A unified graphic design results in a pleasing, effective, and very readable piece. The repetition of pink lines in this invitation creates a distinctive design element. And pink and chocolate brown just happen to be the hottest new color combo.

The Visual Journal

One of the simplest pleasures I can recommend, and one of the most effective ways of developing designs, is to begin keeping a visual journal in which you can experiment with materials, supplies, and techniques to discover and/or enhance your own unique style.

You're probably accustomed to seeing photographs elegantly matted and framed, but effectively combining photographs with decorative papers and embellishments takes some practice—and daring. It may actually feel awkward at first, but once you get into the flow of it, you'll have a ball coming up with combinations that look as if the various elements were designed specifically to complement each other.

Go through your photo archives, cabinets, and drawers and gather diverse items that might work grouped together to convey a theme or color scheme. Even "found objects" such as old buttons, newspaper clippings, and coins can be used to add interest and subtext to your designs. The creative challenge is in finding things that will complement and enhance your photographs rather than become a distraction. Scour your neighborhood art supply store: You might be amazed at the varied selection of embellishments available. Decorative paper scraps, skeleton leaves, and dried flowers also make wonderful elements for a visual journal.

1. Lay out your stuff on a page of a spiral-bound craft album, building up layers. Don't worry about doing it right—take your time and just play. Move things around and see what resonates for you. Don't glue anything down yet.

2. When you're satisfied with the layout, it's time to make it permanent. If you have a digital or Polaroid camera, take a snapshot of the layout to use as a reference guide. Otherwise, make a simple sketch.

3. Now, remove everything and reattach each item, working from the bottom layer up.

You can also experiment with text by adding specimens from magazines, newspapers, and even packaging. Use your computer and printer to explore typography—fonts and font families, character weights or thicknesses, and combinations of typefaces. (See "Working with Type" on page 35 for more about typography.)

Be daring. Make mistakes. This journal is for your eyes only and is meant to help you hone your personal style, which will shine through in the stationery, albums, and other mementos you create.

When I travel, I always try to bring home a few yards of a newly discovered ribbon or several sheets of decorative paper from the local art store, rubber stamp emporium, or scrapbook shop. Overseas travel yields eclectic media, including coins and paper money. Even free tidbits like newspapers and paper bags are candidates for collage.

My penchant for metallics is evident on this journal page that combines decorative paper with sparkling gold detail, gold-and-black metallic string, and some experimental Auratones (see page 61). On the facing page, a white-on-white theme combines embossed paper, seam binding, silk cord, a feather, shells, a Polaroid image transfer (see page 63), and photo corners. I used acrylic gel medium to build up some texture.

Creating Layouts with a Digital-Imaging Program

Just as most of us now have cell phones, computers, and digital cameras, I believe the time will come when "everyone" will also have some version of Adobe Photoshop. It's just too much fun to live without!

Of course, photographers have been flocking to Photoshop in droves for digital imaging—to correct poor exposure, improve colors, remove distractions, and apply creative effects—but most don't realize that they can do far more with Photoshop than edit photos. In this book, we're also going to use Photoshop for simple graphic design.

Photoshop or Photoshop Elements?

That is the question. Theoretically, Elements is for the amateur or home user, and if you're just starting out, Elements is your best bet. It's much less expensive, it makes photo editing easier, it's almost as powerful as the full version, and you won't be intimidated by loads of features you'll probably never use. True, Photoshop has more advanced options for fine tuning and control, but Elements has some handy features that aren't available in Photoshop such as easy red eye removal. I personally use Photoshop, and the exercises and projects in the book were done with Photoshop, but the instructions can be easily adapted for Elements.

Getting Around in Photoshop

When you open a file in Photoshop, you will see a work area with a Toolbox that contains various image-editing tools, a Menu bar organized by tasks, an Options bar that is specific to the selected tool, an Active Image area that displays the open file, and a Palette Well with individual palettes for monitoring and modifying images.

The best way to learn a program is to use it as often as you can. Start off by performing some simple tasks, such as cropping and/or resizing images, converting them to black and white or sepia, and adjusting the tone. (We'll do all of these things and more in Chapter 3.) Every time you use it, try one more tool or feature, exploring its variables and possibilities. Whether you're using Photoshop or Elements, if you're not already familiar with the fundamentals in terms of using the tools and opening and saving files, you might want to take advantage of a beginning workshop in your area, or purchase and use a basic workbook. Take some time to familiarize yourself with the tools used in the projects presented within this book and their keyboard shortcuts (shown in parentheses on the following page).

1. **Toolbox**
2. **Options bar**
3. **Menu bar**
4. **Active image area**
5. **Palette Well**

The Photoshop work area is comprised of an "intuitive" arrangement that makes it easy to create layouts and edit images.

Macintosh Versus PC

I work on a Macintosh, but for all intents and purposes, the Photoshop interface is identical on both Macintosh and Windows platforms. The only discernible difference is in the keyboard shortcuts. To accommodate that difference, when necessary I'll give directions for both in this format: Return/ Enter, with the Mac command preceding the slash and the Windows command following it. If only one shortcut, such as Shift, is given, that means it's the same shortcut for both platforms.

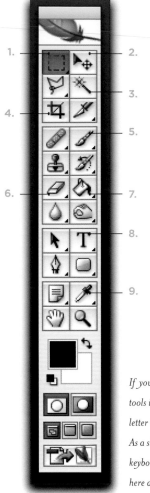

1. **Marquee (M)**
2. **Move (V)**
3. **Magic Wand (W)**
4. **Crop (C)**
5. **Brush (B)**
6. **Eraser (E)**
7. **Paint Bucket/Gradient (G)**
8. **Type (T)**
9. **Eyedropper (I)**

If you pass your cursor over the individual tools in the Photoshop Toolbox, you'll notice a letter in parentheses after the name of the tool. As a shortcut, you can press that letter on the keyboard to access the tool. The tools labeled here are the ones used in this book.

Before Designing a Layout in Photoshop

HERE ARE SOME TIPS THAT WILL START YOU OUT ON THE RIGHT FOOT FOR CREATING DIGITAL LAYOUTS:

- Under the Window menu, make sure Layers is checked.
- In the Toolbox, click on the Move tool (V), and in the Move tool options bar, check Auto Select Layer. Now you can click on any pixel in an open window to activate its particular layer.
- Under the View menu, check Rulers, and check the Snap feature. This will aid in using Guides, which are dragged out from the Rulers, essential elements for accurately aligned layouts. Although Guides show on your monitor, they don't print. You can turn them on and off under the View menu in the sub-menu Show, or press Command/ Control + ;.

Working with Layers

The seemingly humble Layers feature is one of the most powerful and important aspects of Photoshop, allowing you to make any number of corrections at any time without affecting the underlying layers. Layers are managed through the Layers palette. We'll use layers in most of the project in the book, which will help you become familiar with using them.

When you work in layers, you can clean up on one layer, improve contrast or tone on another, add text on another. It's a good idea to save the layered file in case you need to make any changes to a specific layer. Then flatten the layers (Layers>Flatten Image) and save the file under a new name. Flattened files are easier to cut and paste and are also very useful when "ganging" more than one layout onto a page for printing (e.g., two invitations).

Basic Steps

To create a layout containing an image and text in Adobe Photoshop, it's as simple as 1, 2, 3, 4, 5, and 6!

1. Choose File>New and select or create a custom size that conforms to the *intended*, or finished, size of your piece.

2. Go to File>Page Setup and select or create a setup that conforms to the *actual* size of your paper or card stock. It's often easiest to use letter-size paper and then trim it after printing. Designate the proper printing orientation.

3. Open an image file. If you have previously added layers in Photoshop, be sure to flatten them. Choose Select>All, then Edit>Copy. Close the image file without saving it.

4. Return to the new file by clicking on the window and go to Edit>Paste. The image will appear in the middle of the layout; use the Move tool (V) to reposition it. Note that in the Layers palette, the image is on its own layer; you can edit it, move it, or resize it at any time by first clicking on that layer.

TIP

A simple and fast alternative to cutting and pasting is to simply click and drag the image from one file into another. Make sure the Move tool is activated first.

5. Select the Type tool (T) and type the text. Note that, as with the image, the text is in its own layer in the Layers palette; you can edit it, move it, or resize it at any time by first clicking on that layer. Use the arrow keys to move it; double-click on the T thumbnail in the Layers palette to edit or resize it.

TIP

To add a new line of text close to an area that already has text, choose the Type tool, hold down the Shift key, then click on the layout. (If you don't hold down the Shift key, the Type tool will select the text that's already there.)

6. Save the file.

To create a layout, follow the steps under "Basic Steps" to open a new file and "toss in" the basics, with each element on its own layer.

Refine the layout by changing the font, resizing the graphics, and moving things around. Dragging out Guides to delineate the horizontal and vertical center and a $1/2$-inch border all around makes it easy to create this conventional centered layout.

Experiment with basic concepts of graphic design to create a more advanced layout. Here a colored background was added. The final layout has a better sense of flow.

Resizing an Image

If the image is in its own separate file with no other layers, go to Select>All, then Edit>Free Transform. If the image exists within a layered file, activate the image's layer, use the Rectangular Marquee tool to select the image, then go to Edit>Free Transform.

Resize the photo by either entering percentages in the width and height boxes in the Options bar (e.g., 50 percent in each box to make it half as large) or by dragging a handle. To avoid changing the proportions, hold down the Shift key while dragging.

Press Return/Enter to apply the transformation.

Managing Text

It's a good idea to type groups of related information (e.g., names, date and time, street address and city) on separate layers so that you have the ability to edit or move them independently. To do that, once you've finished typing the first item or grouping, click on the Move tool, click on the Type tool again, then click on the open window, and a new layer will be created. Follow that process for each additional component.

To edit text—for example, to change the font or point size—highlight the appropriate layer in the Layers palette, and, with the Type tool activated, drag across the text to select it, or simply double-click on the text layer thumbnail in the Layers palette, then make the appropriate changes. Use the Type Options bar as well as the Character palette to finesse the text (e.g., alignment, color, and spacing).

Making Digital Templates

Create a new folder called "Templates," and each time you generate a new design layout, save a layered version in that folder with an apt designation (e.g., 5 x 5 Template, Folio Template). Then, to begin a new project utilizing an existing layout, open the appropriate template. Immediately rename and save it in a folder for that particular project (e.g., Jones Invitation), thereby maintaining the original template with its original name intact. Make the pertinent changes to the *new* file (e.g., highlighting the text and modifying it, substituting fonts, swapping images) and then save that file in both layered and flattened formats. (As with any digital endeavor, it's always a good idea to periodically save your work as you progress.)

TIP

Always print rough drafts on plain paper, tweak the layout to perfection, and *then* print on your good paper.

Working with Type

Even when combined with a photograph, text is usually the most important element of a printed piece as it communicates pertinent information. It also conveys subtle messages, such as wit, playfulness, sophistication, and even rebellion (witness the countless "grunge" fonts springing up everywhere on the Internet). To be effective, the text in your piece should be:

- Readable: Extensive text must be easy to read, and short stand-alone segments of text must be capable of being quickly deciphered.
- Appropriate: The text should echo the personality of the individual or event at hand.
- Visually appealing: Create contrast and interest through the use of dissimilar but complementary typefaces—usually no more than two for our purposes—and/or point sizes.
- Free of errors: How many times have you been turned off to a purveyor of goods or services because they're printed materials were shoddy? Okay, that was on purpose. But the point is, you can't rely on spell check! *There, their*, and *they're* are all spelled correctly but have entirely different meanings.

Font Categories

Typography—the art and craft of designing typefaces and arranging type for display—was at one time the domain of a very specialized group of highly skilled designers and typesetters, but with the advent of the World Wide Web, there are now thousands of fonts available to the layperson. Although you *could* stick with the default fonts on your computer, you might want to round out your selection with a few carefully chosen styles.

There are five basic font categories. For the sake of diversity, you should have at least two typefaces from each, plus some decorative styles and elements to add charm and personality to your printed pieces. Bear in mind that most fonts come in families of varying weights (e.g., light, bold, heavy) and italics, which can dramatically affect their look and feel.

> ### TIP
> If you end up with an extensive font menu, say in excess of two hundred typefaces, you'll probably want a font management program, such as Font Reserve. A font manager allows you to preview fonts and to reduce font overload by activating and deactivating fonts as needed.

CLASSIC OLD STYLE

Conservative, very readable, with well-defined serifs (the little hooks on the ends of characters) and subtle contrast in weight from thick to thin strokes. Commonly used old-style fonts include Book Antigua, Caslon, Garamond, Goudy Old Style, and Times New Roman.

SANS SERIF

"Sans" means "without"; ergo, sans serif fonts don't have 'em. Commonly used sans serif fonts are Arial, Avant Garde, Bank Gothic, Bauhaus, Futura, and Gill Sans.

MODERN

The opposite of old style, these fonts have more attitude and are often used to add character rather than readability (although some moderns such as Monotype are very readable). Typically featuring stark contrast between light and heavy strokes, their serifs are lighter, often just thin horizontal lines. Bodoni is the most commonly used modern; Fenice and Onyx are two more examples.

SLAB SERIF

Simple, sturdy, with heavy squared-off serifs and minimal stroke variation, slab serifs are reminiscent of manual typewriters and old newspapers and are enjoying new popularity as such in retro applications. Commonly used slab serifs are Clarendon, Boton, and Courier, and several "typewriter" and "letterpress" fonts, such as Letterpress Text and P22 Typewriter.

SCRIPT

Whether traditional or contemporary, script faces emulate handwriting and are a must if you're going to be designing social stationery with any degree of regularity. They're indispensable as a contrast to the other categories of type, and their number is rapidly growing. Bickley Script, Liana, Mistral, and Prince Charming are a few script fonts.

Try choosing two or more fonts that are VERY different from each other yet somehow work together. Add photos and scanned backgrounds. Print your "font flags," then paste them in your visual journal for a ready reference guide when the time comes to design a layout for your newest project.

Fanciful Fonts

Adorn your layouts with decorative fonts, dingbats and ornaments. They're real attention grabbers, and they're fun to use.

DECORATIVE FONTS

Artistic typefaces created by font designers, decorative typestyles are as diverse as personalities. They're rarely suitable for extensive reading and should be used sparingly—a little goes a long way. Try a decorative font for an oversized initial capital letter. A few examples are Bernard Fashion ICG, Papyrus ICG, and P22 Cezanne.

DINGBATS AND ORNAMENTS

Often contained in font sets, these characters are actually decorative elements that can be used to add a graphic theme or to unify a layout—for instance, as bullets or borders (when strung together). They're not only practical but lots of fun to use. Zapf Dingbats, Nat Vignette Ornaments, and P22 Art Nouveau Extras are a few examples.

> ## TIP
>
> If you find you're really drawn to the art of typography (as I am), you'll probably want to check out "expert sets" containing special characters such as ligatures, swashes, small caps, and old-style figures. Such characters can add a distinctly professional flair to printed pieces.

Adjusting Spacing: Kerning and Leading and Tracking—Oh, My!

Kerning is the manual adjustment of the space between two individual letters or characters. *Tracking* is very similar to kerning but is generally applied to a larger range of characters. *Leading* (as in a piece of metal, as was once used to set type) is the space between lines of type.

In Photoshop, there is a "hidden" feature with which you can control all of the above and more. When you select the Type tool, if

you look near the right end of the Options bar, you'll see a little box that looks something like a sheet of paper. If you pass your cursor over it, you'll see the words "Toggle the Character and Paragraph Palettes." Click, and choose the Character palette. Ta-da!

You now have the ability to control all aspects of spacing related to type. Now, you may not want to go there—it takes time and some practice to finesse type—but isn't it nice to know you can?

The Character palette gives you additional font and text control well beyond the Options bar.

Creating Warped Text

If you pass your cursor over the little box that shows a T over an arch near the end of the Type Options bar, you'll see the words "Create Warped Text." There are a few styles of "warpage" that are particularly well suited to children's birthday party invitations and other informal pieces. Try Arc to complement a round or oval image graphic, Flag or Wave to give the impression of a ribbon or banner. You can even tweak the bend as well as the horizontal and vertical distortion. (Note: The Warp tool can only be accessed when you are in an open window and have activated the Type tool.)

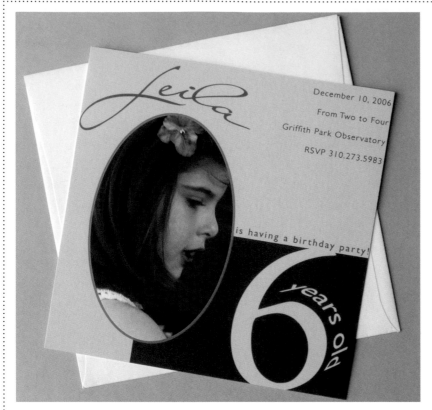

The Warp tool allows you to design your own cards and invitations to rival those found in stationery stores. (Fonts: Liana and Gill Sans)

Some Excellent Typographic Links

Here's a list of my favorite font-related websites. Fonts are not only fun, but having a well-stocked library of typefaces is an imperative if designing stationery is to be a significant part of your life.

MyFonts.com
A useful and user-friendly site where you can identify, find, test drive, and purchase fonts.

Émigre.com
An independent type foundry that's always on the cutting edge—even their catalogs are collectibles. It's all about the art, with font philosophy, interviews with type designers, essays, posters—great stuff!

Identifont.com
An amazing resource with which you can identify

a font by answering a series of simple questions about its appearance. In addition, Identifont now offers "Fontifier": You simply print out a form, fill it in, scan it, upload it, and—for only $9!—receive a font of your own handwriting. The site also has some free fonts.

P22.com
Not just a type foundry but a virtual typographic community with fonts, mugs, T-shirts, books, posters, and more. For true fontophiles.

TypoFile (www.will-harris.com)
It's like having an uncle in the font business. A must-visit site for information, inspiration, and, yes, more fonts!

Adding Color to Your Layouts

You needn't be content with black type or a plain white background. Add color to complement a photograph, to echo the color of a mailing envelope or embellishment, or to suggest the occasion or season. Here are some methods for adding color to your layout.

Changing the Type Color

Use colored type to add energy, emphasis, contrast, and mood to a layout.

METHOD 1

Here's how easy it is to select a color, any color.

1. In the Layers palette, double-click on the T thumbnail in the layer containing the text.

2. In the Toolbox, click on the foreground color swatch and, in the Color Picker dialog box, choose the color you want.

3. Click OK, then click on another tool (e.g., the Move tool) to deselect the type.

METHOD 2

You can also match a color in a particular photograph to complement it.

1. Use the Eyedropper tool to "sample," or take, a color pixel from a photograph. The foreground color in the Toolbox will change to that color.

2. In the Layers palette, double-click on the T thumbnail in the layer containing the text you wish to change.

3. Click on the foreground color in the Toolbox, then click OK in the Color Picker dialog box.

4. Click on another tool (e.g., the Move tool) to deselect the type.

Outlining the Type with a Different Color

To create more contrast, or just for fun, you can also outline type with a different color.

1. In the Layers palette, double-click on the

T thumbnail in the layer containing the text you wish to outline.

2. Go to Layer>Layer Style>Stroke and choose a size, a color, and a position (usually "outside"). You can also adjust the opacity. Click OK.

Filling Open-Face Type with Color

Fonts suitable for filling include Caslon Open Face, Myriad Sketch, Cloister, Desdemona, and Interlude (its uppercase characters only). Here's how to do it:

1. Open a new file, choose a font, and type some text. It's easiest to use a large point size; you can resize it later.

2. In the Layers palette, create a new layer above the text layer.

3. With the text layer active, to create a selection, click on the Magic Wand tool, then click on the interior of the open-faced letter or letters you wish to fill. You can add to the selection by pressing Shift and at the same time clicking other open areas with the Magic Wand tool. (Contiguous should be checked in the Options bar; set the Tolerance to 8.)

4. Choose a color from the Swatch palette or by clicking on the Foreground color in the Toolbox and using the Color Picker. You can also use the Eyedropper tool to "sample" a color from a photograph.

5. Click on the new layer. Make sure the foreground color in the Toolbox is the correct color, choose the Brush tool, then paint inside the letters. Select a large brush to paint several letters at once. (By painting on a separate layer, you can delete it or change the color at any time, unless or until the file is flattened.) Go to Select>Deselect.

6. If the text needs to be resized, with both layers selected or merged, go to Edit>Transform>Scale and either drag the handles (hold down the Shift key to maintain the height/width ratio) or enter percentages in the options bar. Press Return/Enter to apply the transformation.

Colored type is fun and eye-catching. (Font: Stencil)

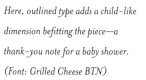

Here, outlined type adds a child-like dimension befitting the piece—a thank-you note for a baby shower. (Font: Grilled Cheese BTN)

Fill open-face type with color for an attention-grabbing effect. (Fonts: Liana and Interlude)

Filling Type with a Photo or Pattern

Here's a Photoshop technique that's SO much fun to do—and it really enhances the WOW factor of a custom piece! It works best with a "fat" font—try Bauhaus Heavy, Gill Sans Extra Bold, Stencil, or Brush Script—and just one or two words with a large font size. (See page 146 for an example of a card that uses type filled with a photo.)

1. Open a new file. Type some text with the font of your choice.

2. Open an image file and drag it into the new file.

3. Make sure the image layer is above the text layer in the Layers palette, and click on the line between the two layers while holding down the Option/Alt key. Voilá—the photo now fills the letters! (It may take a couple tries.)

4. In the window, use the Move tool (V) to position the image where you want it within the type.

5. Experiment by changing the size of the font or resizing the image.

To create the pattern used to fill this type, I simply scanned some handmade paper. (Font: Grilled Cheese BTN)

Adding a Background Color

You can also dress up your layout by adding a background color. In the Layers palette, create a new layer, then use the Paint Bucket or the Gradient tool to drop in a color or color range. You can drag the layer to where you want it in the Layers palette and adjust the opacity of the layer to lighten the color.

Adding a Colorful "Mat"

Another method to add color is to create a digital "mat" by inserting a block or shape filled with color. To do this, first create a new layer. With that layer active, use the Marquee tool to create a shape, then fill it with color via the Paint Bucket or Gradient tool. Use the Move tool to place it in the correct position. You may also have to drag the layer in the Layers palette to place it behind the proper element(s) in your layout. To create a three-dimensional effect, go to Layer Style Blending Options and add a drop shadow.

Digital "mats" replicate the use of matboard for framing a photograph. (Font: Bickley Script)

CHAPTER 3

Creative Photo Techniques

In this chapter we will explore several tantalizing traditional, computer-based, and alternative fine art techniques to add pizzazz to your projects. But before we kick up our heels, let's take a few moments to address what lies at the heart of every project in this book—and that is, of course, the photograph.

Composing Better Photos

You should already be familiar with your own camera (read the manual again—you might be amazed at what you discover!) and the basics of photography. In this section, we'll focus on composition and some special techniques you can use to add interest and subtext to your photos.

Content and composition are the most important qualities of an image. In photography, content, or subject matter, is usually the first line of response, but composition, or design, runs a close second. The intentional use of specific design principles will add to a photograph's effectiveness both visually and emotionally.

A pleasing visual design owes its success to the appropriate use of line, shape, color, texture, size, and/or spatial relationships. Those elements can also be used to draw the viewer beneath the surface of an image. Incorporating these visual elements of design in your compositions will ensure that each shot is more than merely a literal translation of what you are seeing. This is how the artist steals the stage from the technician.

Line

A line, whether actual (as a horizon or road) or implied (as the direction in which someone is looking), forms a path for the viewer's eye, or imagination, to travel. A diagonal or curving line creates more of a sense of motion than a horizontal or vertical line.

Shape

When lines meet, a shape is formed. A geometric or organic (natural) shape creates positive space surrounded by negative space, the area around the shape. When photographing pregnant women in particular, the interplay between negative and positive shapes is beautifully apparent. Using light and shadow to accentuate them adds to the dramatic effect.

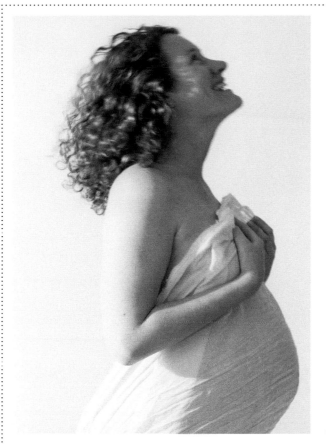

The line implied by a simple upward gaze makes us think of heavenly matters, especially appropriate when considering the miracle of life.

Natural curves create a balance of positive and negative shapes.

Texture

A sense of texture lends a tactile quality to an image. Think about the sensory contrast between swirling silk and nubby knits, mature and newborn skin, sand and water. Focus on texture to add a layer of feeling.

NIK Software filters were used to create three distinctly different color effects, with artistic license reigning over realism. From DIREX: original, unfiltered color; Monday Morning Sepia; BW Conversion—Tonal Enhancer; Duplex Monochrome.

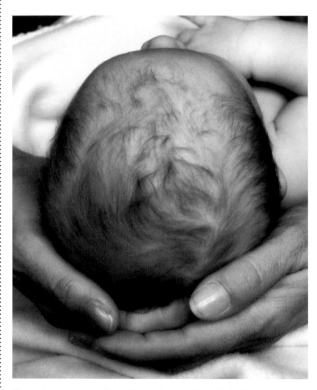

The newborn's porcelain skin and downy head gently cradled in her mother's hands provide a study in textural contrast.

Color

Color, or the absence thereof, may have the most dramatic impact on an image. Its effect is immediate. Whether realistic color, altered color, black and white, or toned, each mode suggests a different mood and offers an opportunity for creative interpretation of the event or subject.

Size

Nowhere within the realm of photography is the element of size as irresistible and exhilarating to use as it is in photographing pregnant women, babies, and children. Size does matter! A photograph of a woman who is eight months pregnant tells a much different story than that of a woman at four months along. What better way to communicate the awe-inspiring miracle of life than with an image of a newborn's hand grasping an adult's finger? In this context, the opportunities for using size to tell a story are seemingly endless.

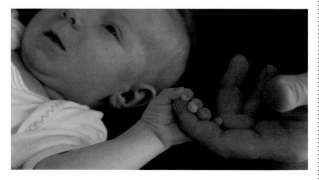

Using size to tell a story. (See "Toning" on page 51 for instructions on creating a sepia-toned image like this one.)

Spatial Relationships

Spatial relationships create depth. Use your lens aperture in conjunction with its focal length to control the depth of field to render a background or foreground out of focus, or include a small shape in the distance or a large shape in the foreground to underscore the element of space. The interplay between light and shadow can also contribute to the sense of spatial relationships within a setting.

A shallow focal length creates a sense of depth while keeping our attention focused on the heart of the matter.

More Creative Ideas

There are other nontechnical techniques you can use to add interest to your photos. Take the angle, or vantage point, into consideration. A direct approach tells a straightforward story, while an unusual or exaggerated angle communicates a subtle message. Indirect angles evoke a photojournalistic or documentary style

of storytelling, instilling a sense of being there. Shooting up at or down on a subject emphasizes not only size but power (up) or vulnerability (down). Shooting at a raked, or tilted, angle conveys an offbeat interpretation and adds a sense of motion. And speaking of motion, the repetition of lines, shapes, or colors within an image causes our eye to move back and forth, adding a sense of motion. Blur, of course, whether intentional or not, also lets us know there is movement. Life, especially family life, does not stand still.

He may be rough and tumble, but he still believes in the Easter bunny. Shooting down on this little guy gives us a sense of his vulnerability.

Contrast

The difference in the amount of light between highlights and shadows in a photograph constitutes contrast and is controlled by film speed or ISO equivalent (in a digital camera), the size of the lens aperture, and the shutter speed.

You can also introduce a subtext of emotional/perceptual contrast in such ways as photographing a typically colorful scene (e.g., a birthday party at a theme park or the family in front of a Christmas tree) with a black-and-white treatment, by giving a potentially sad or disturbing image (e.g., a pensive or crying child) a beautiful treatment, or by bringing something typically hidden (e.g., the pregnant form) into sharp focus.

Contrast can also be seen in the opposition of curved and straight lines, positive and negative space, and smooth and rough textures. Contrast usually results in a sense of balance. Balance can be distributed symmetrically or asymmetrically, which is often more dynamic and interesting.

Some of the shadowy mystery of childhood is captured in this thoughtful study. The pensive quality is offset by the quirky garb: pj's, a tutu, and fleece-lined boots.

Tousled hair, breakfast cereal, and morning light add up to an authentic child-hood moment. The tight crop transforms the chair backs into a rhythmic pattern.

Framing and Cropping

You can choose exactly what to place within the boundary of your photograph, cropping in camera. Attention will be drawn to that area where the object or objects are most clearly focused and therefore prominent; that's where the viewer's eye will first go.

Whenever possible, take both a long shot and a close-up. Then get even closer. Yes, it's now as easy as pie to crop a photograph in a digital imaging program (see "Cropping" on page 49), but bear in mind that there is also the potential for loss of clarity when that cropped image is enlarged.

A Few More Tips

- Be sure to include any naturally occurring "frames" within your viewfinder, such as overhanging trees, windows, and doors.
- Notice the quality of light. If it's harsh, use flash as fill, or move the subject closer to a wall that can be used for reflection or to an area of open shade like that found under a covered porch; if it's too shadowy, move the subject next to a window, or use fill flash.
- Whenever you're shooting on location, be sure to check out the background—chances are it's busy and distracting. This can kill an otherwise great shot. Either throw that background out of focus with a long lens or a shallow depth of field, or create a black-and-white image to lessen the distraction.

Digital Darkroom Techniques

Adobe Photoshop is the photographer's best friend—a photo lab in a box, a digital darkroom. No smelly or toxic chemicals, no need to work in absolute darkness, no shutting yourself off from the world. Well, come to think of it, many of us do end up spending untold hours immersed in Photoshop—mostly because we simply enjoy experimenting and tweaking to suit our vision. So roll up your sleeves and join in the fun!

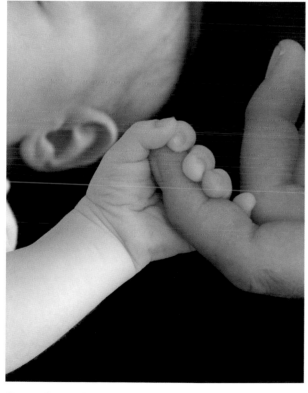

Cropping this image distills it to its most essential elements.

(See the original image on page 46.)

NOTE

Get into the habit of saving your file under a new name *before making any changes*. You don't want to alter your original photo.

Cropping

One of the most important and effective methods for dramatically improving a photograph is to crop it, thereby removing extraneous or distracting detail, enhancing composition, and directing attention to the emotional content of the image.

1. Open the image that you'd like to crop and save the file under a new name.

2. Press C to access the Crop tool.

3. Click and drag the Crop tool over the area you wish to keep.

- For a square crop, hold down the Shift key as you drag.
- To move the selection (or "marquee"), place the pointer inside the bounding box and drag.
- To change the size while keeping the proportions the same, hold down the Shift key as you drag a corner handle.
- To crop and resize the image simultaneously, first enter a height, width, and resolution in the Options bar.

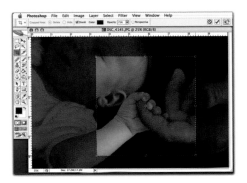

The dark area outside the dotted lines is the portion of the photo that will be removed once you have completed the crop procedure.

4. When you find a pleasing crop, press Return/Enter, then save the file.

Converting a Color Image to Black and White

There are lots of good reasons for converting a color image to black and white. The most common among them is that black-and-white images often seem more expressive than color, perhaps because the absence of color allows for a more subjective interpretation. Sometimes the transformation can add a fine art or photo-journalistic appearance. It also tends to lessen distractions, and it improves the appearance of ruddy or discolored skin.

In Photoshop, you can simply convert the file to grayscale, but the result is often dull and lifeless. Here are a couple better methods that will give you improved tonal quality, the hallmark of a good black-and-white photo-graph. Try desaturating the photo (Image>Adjustments>Desaturate), then adjusting the Levels sliders (Image>Adjustments>Levels). Here's another method I often use...but be sure to experiment to see which method gives you the best tones, as results will vary from one image to another.

1. Open a color (RGB) image that you want to convert to black and white and save the file under a new name. (If the image is in CMYK mode, change the mode to RGB Color. Go to Image>Mode>RGB Color.)

2. In the Channels palette, notice that the thumbnail next to the RGB channel appears in full color, and the thumbnails next to the individual channels of Red, Green, and Blue are displayed in black and white.

   Click to isolate each channel in turn to see which one looks best as a black-and-white image; they'll appear on-screen in grayscale. Most likely, one will be too dark, one will be too light, and one will be just about right.

3. With the optimal channel highlighted, click on the Channel palette's drop-down menu

(the little right-facing triangle in the upper right-hand corner) and choose Duplicate Channel. In the new dialog box that appears, under the Document drop-down menu, choose New. Click OK.

4. You now have a new document containing a black-and-white image. In the Image menu, under Mode, choose Grayscale, and save the file.

The color image is fine but a little too realistic for my taste . . .

. . . while converting it to black and white gives it a more artistic interpretation.

Toning

Applying a sepia tone to an image conveys the look and feel of an old photograph. Toning with color adds interest and can also convey emotion. In the early days of photography, silver halide images were toned to achieve archival stability, but the side effect of expressiveness is something we can emulate today simply to create a subtle mood in our own photos. Here are some simple methods for creating a toned image in Photoshop.

1. Open a color (RGB) image and save the file under a new name. To transform a black-and-white (Grayscale) image into a toned image, first convert it to RGB mode (Image>Mode>RGB Color).

2. Go to Image>Adjustments>Hue/Saturation. Make sure Preview is checked, click on the Colorize box, then move the Hue slider until you find a tone you like. You can also adjust the Saturation and Lightness if you wish, although it's usually not necessary.

TIP

If you perform the colorizing on an adjustment layer (Layer>New>Adjustment Layer>Hue/Saturation), you can access this layer at any time (until and unless the layers are flattened) to make further adjustments to the settings.

3. Save the file.

Giving this photo a sepia tone adds a sense of warmth and timelessness.

Adding Borders

Adding a border not only makes an image stand out, but, depending on the type of border, affects the overall look of a piece. Adding a border characteristic of a specific type of film, negative, or process (e.g, Polaroid image transfer) gives an image a certain fine art panache.

A smooth border adds definition . . .

. . . while a spattered border adds interest.

THE STROKE METHOD

Here's the simplest way to add a border in Photoshop:

1. Open an image file and save it under a different name.

2. Go to Select>All, then Edit>Stroke. Choose a border width (in pixels), color, and location (usually inside). You may want to experiment with the Blending mode and Opacity options. When you're satisfied, click OK and save the file.

THE BORDER SELECTION METHOD

This method allows you to choose a smooth or textured brush to create a border.

1. Open an image file and save it under a different name.

2. Go to Select>All, then Select>Modify>Border. Choose a border width (in pixels).

3. In the Toolbox, select a Foreground color.

4. Click on the Brush tool (B) and select a brush from the Preset Picker in the Options bar. Try a spatter brush or dry brush. (If you don't find one you like, click on the right-facing triangle to load more Brush presets.) Now just paint in the border. Using this method you'll never color outside the lines! Have fun experimenting with opacity and blending modes.

5. Save the file.

THE BORROWED BORDERS METHOD

You may also want to experiment with some of the free borders you can download from my website www.bsmithphotography.com/borders. Just click to select a border, then save it to your desktop or elsewhere. Follow these steps to apply it to an image.

1. Open an image file, and save it under a new name.

2. Open the file containing the border you've selected.

3. Use the Move tool (V) to click on the edge of the border and drag it into the image file.

4. With the border layer highlighted in the Layers palette, go to Edit>Transform>Scale and drag the handles until the border is the same size as the photograph. Click Return/ Enter to apply the transformation and save the file.

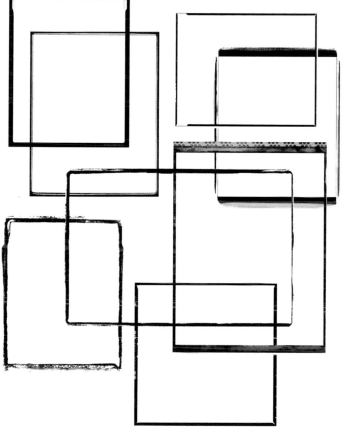

Feel free to borrow these borders (for your personal projects only, please).

It's definitely cheating, but adding this border with the notched corners makes the image look as if it were shot with a very expensive medium-format Hasselblad camera.

Turning Your Photos into Works of Art

Even if you're not a "paint" artist—if you don't paint original pieces of art from scratch—you can enjoy the considerable excitement, satisfaction, and fun derived from creating painterly images. And if, like me, you're intimidated by the thought of a blank canvas, you'll soon have the tools to confidently fill that canvas with your own creative self-expression.

Spot Coloring or Tinting

You've undoubtedly seen greeting cards, calendars, books, and posters featuring a vintage hand-colored style. It's a popular look, and many photographers today spend hours and hours with paints and cotton swabs creating beautiful fine art prints. Now you can emulate the look in Photoshop—without the mess, and without any knowledge of paint or painting techniques. Best of all, you'll use the colors of the original photograph, so there's absolutely no guesswork when it comes to "mixing" colors. You might want to tint the entire image, or just do some spot coloring.

The original image . . .

. . . with an overall tinted effect . . .

. . . and with selective spot coloring.

1. Start with a color image and save the file under a new name.

2. Go to Layer>New>Layer via Copy.

3. Choose Image>Adjustments>Desaturate.

4. With the new layer highlighted, click on the Add Layer Mask icon (the rectangle with a circle in the middle) at the bottom of the Layers palette. Click on the Layer Mask thumbnail in the Layers palette to activate it.

5. In the Toolbox, make sure the foreground color is black (press X or click on the little curved arrows to the top right of the large color swatches in the Toolbox).

6. Using a soft Brush (press B or click on the icon in the Toolbox), "paint" over the area you would like to reveal. The color from the underlying layer will appear. For a subtler effect, lower the opacity of the brush on the Options bar. Zoom (Command/Ctrl +/−) in and out as necessary and vary the size of the Brush as you work for increased maneuverability. Switch the foreground color to white to "erase" any mistakes, then back to black to continue revealing color.

7. Save the file.

Sketching in Photoshop

Here's a great way to use Photoshop to turn a photograph into what looks like a detailed sketch. It's easy, it's fun, and it's the perfect technique to use if you're making a photo gift book and don't want the images to look exactly like photographs—say, for a keepsake of a child's birthday party or other special event. It also works particularly well with scenic and architectural subject matter.

Using the "find edges" technique transformed this photo into a sketch–like piece of art.

1. Open an image file, save under a different name, and duplicate the background layer (Layer>Duplicate Layer>OK).

2. With the duplicate layer highlighted in the Layers palette, go to Filter>Stylize> Find Edges.

3. In the Layers palette, change the blending mode for the duplicate layer from Normal to Overlay.

4. (Opt.) Add a Levels adjustment layer and/or a Hue/Saturation adjustment layer and play with the settings.

TIP

With adjustment layers, you can click on their icons in the Layers palette to go back in and make further adjustments until and unless the layers are flattened.

5. Save the file.

Channel Mixing

For some totally wild and unexpected color shifts, experiment with channel mixing. It's pretty much hit or miss, but it's lots of fun to play with. This technique also works well on an image that has already undergone some kind of intermediate transformation, be it Polaroid image transfer (see page 63) or the digital sketch technique detailed above, where the integrity of skin tones is not critical.

1. Open an image file (RGB), duplicate it
   (Image>Duplicate>OK), and save under a
   new name. Close the original file.

2. In the Channels palette, click on the drop-
   down menu (the little right-facing triangle
   in the upper right-hand corner) and choose
   Split Channels. As you can see, your color
   image has been replaced by three new grayscale images, each with a different
   color designation.

3. With any of the three images active, choose
   Merge Channels from the Channels palette
   menu. In the dialog box that opens, the
   Mode should be RGB Color and the number
   of Channels should be 3. Click OK.

4. In the Merge RGB Channels dialog box that
   opens, reassign the channel specifications
   by opening each window in turn and "shuf-
   fling" the colors. For example, choose Blue
   for the Red channel, Red for the Green
   channel, and Green for the Blue channel.
   Results will vary wildly depending on
   the reassignments.

5. Save the resulting version of your choice.

*The fantasy element of this particular image lends itself to creative interpretation
via various channel mixes.*

Adding Textures and Backgrounds

You can add photos and scans of textures and backgrounds to your personal stock photo library and use them as digital layers. Once you start collecting textured backgrounds for your stock library, the way you look at the world is bound to change. You'll see beauty and potential in rusty metal, peeling paint, crumpled paper, even debris. Adding a textured layer can change the overall effect of a photograph, adding depth or making it appear old, distressed, or simply more interesting.

In Photoshop, copy and paste or click and drag a textured background image (with the same mode [usually RGB] and resolution [usually 300 ppi]) into the window containing a photograph. Adjust the opacity of the new layer to your liking, and experiment with the layer blending modes. You can also add a layer mask and use the Brush tool to increase and/or reduce the amount of texture that shows through in particular areas. By working with a layer mask, you can click on its thumbnail to go back into the mask at any time (until and unless the layers are flattened) to tweak the image.

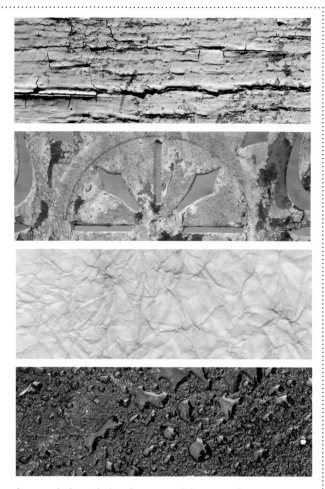

Interesting backgrounds abound in unexpected places . . . peeling paint, rusty surfaces, old paper, even gemlike drops of oil on gravel.

Using Layer Masks

A layer mask is essentially a black-and-white duplicate layer. You can paint on the mask in black, white, or gray. Painting in black allows the underlying image to show through; painting in white hides the underlying image; painting in any shade of gray affects the opacity. By adding a layer mask, you can return at any time (until and unless the layers are flattened) to continue to reveal or eliminate areas of color by first single clicking on the Layer Mask thumbnail in the Layers palette.

This photo was taken under an old pier. I love the shafts of sunlight streaming down. To increase the overall "crusty" effect, I added a textured background of peeling paint, changed the layer blending mode to Overlay, lowered the opacity, and then added a layer mask where I erased the texture effect in the areas containing skin.

Nik Filters

There are lots of ways to give your digital images a painterly quality without adding paint. Photoshop has several interesting filters, but in my opinion, nothing compares to Nik Software. Nik Color Efex Pro 2.0 contains two sets of filters—traditional and stylizing—seventy-five in all, and the program allows you to control the portion of the image that is affected and by how much. Go to www.niksoftware.com to take a test drive. (See page 46 for examples of the use of Nik filters.)

Mixed-media Techniques

It's time to let your inner artist come out and play by using fine art materials and techniques to take your images to another level. Haul out those art supplies buried in the closet; you've been waiting for the right time to experiment, and this is it. Bear in mind that making art takes time . . . time to consider, time to feel. To create your own masterpieces, build up layers slowly, allowing time for your creative process to evolve. This is the beginning of an exciting adventure!

Underprinting

Underprinting is the process of making a digital print and then enhancing it by applying other media such as watercolor paint, pencil, chalk, pastel, or collage materials. It's a bona fide technique, and, although it may have met with some initial resistance, pieces that began with a digital underprint are now found in art galleries and private collections throughout the world.

In Photoshop, you can underprint a pale, "screened-back" version of your image to be completely covered by other media. Go to Select>All, then Image>Adjustments>Hue/ Saturation, and adjust the Lightness slider. Alternatively, you can print it normally and then use other media to add interesting details, accents, and/or highlights. Either way, before printing, you may want to apply a Gaussian Blur to give the image a softer less realistic effect. Go to Filter>Blur>Gaussian Blur, make sure the Preview button is checked, and set the radius to your liking.

To prepare this image, I lightened it with a Hue/Saturation adjustment and printed it on Arches Aquarelle watercolor paper.

I then "painted" the underprint using Derwent watercolor pencils in conjunction with wet brushes.

Printing on Fine Art Paper

Sometimes the substrate itself transforms a photograph into a piece of art. Today there is a wide selection of digital fine art papers—including Epson photo papers, Arches Infinity, Somerset Photo Enhanced Velvet, Hahnemuhle Lumijet, and Crane's Museo—coated specifically for inkjet printers to produce beautiful clarity and tone. Each has a particular texture, sheen, and thickness that must be taken into consideration in terms of the look and intended use of the finished product. Some images cry out for a rough textured surface; others for a smooth glossy treatment. It's imperative to adjust your print settings to match the paper you select, as each paper has specific printer profiles.

Hiromi Paper (www.hiromipaper.com) carries Japanese digital papers that are 100 percent acid free, archival, and coated for inkjet printing. You're not likely to get the same clarity as with the papers mentioned above, but the texture and color of these papers adds considerably to the fine art look and feel of the print.

The texture of Hiromi Peacock paper imparts an interesting sheen that changes with the lighting conditions.

Auratones

I've long been drawn to the gleam of precious metals. The first time I saw one of Edward S. Curtis's *orotones*—an early photographic technique involving a glass plate negative, banana oil, and gold powder—I was smitten and immediately set about trying to create a similar effect. I began by experimenting with materials and techniques at hand—for instance, using glass as the substrate for a Polaroid emulsion lift, then backing it with gold paper or card stock or painstakingly adhering bits of gold leaf. Nothing really resonated.

Then, one morning while in the shower, inspiration struck (as so often happens), and I quickly dried off, knowing I was onto something. I rushed to my desk and hurriedly printed a black-and-white image onto a transparency sheet and then raced to my worktable and grabbed a bottle of liquid gold leaf and a brush, my hand literally shaking with excitement. I painted the "back" of the photo and knew before I had even turned it over to view the results that I had literally struck gold. The Auratone™ was born!

Keep in mind that it's impossible for a photograph of an Auratone to capture the subtle depth and gleam of gold. Make one and you'll see what I mean. (To order a kit, go to www.bsmithphotography.com/.auratonekit.)

The appeal of the Auratone lies in the way it captures light. As Josh Russell wrote of the daguerreotype in his book Yellow Jack, *"Tilt it one way and you see the past, tilt it another and you see the present."*

You Will Need

- Black-and-white digital photo
- 3M transparency film
- Clear clipboard
- Liquid gold leaf
- Jar lid or paint tray
- Sponge brush

1. In Photoshop, flip a black-and-white photograph so that it will print backward (Image>Rotate Canvas>Flip Canvas Horizontal). It will read properly when turned over.

2. Print the image on the textured surface of a sheet of 3M transparency film.

3. Secure the transparency to the clipboard, *textured surface facing up*.

4. Working in a well-ventilated area, pour an adequate amount of gold leaf into a jar lid or other container.

TIP

Pour just enough liquid gold leaf into your container to coat the photograph. It tends to dry up quickly, and you can always add more.

5. Saturate the bottom edge of a foam brush with gold leaf and daub, or stipple, over the image until it is completely covered. Avoid strokes as they will show and are impossible to remove.

6. Hold the clipboard up to the light to see any areas you might have missed. Daub as needed.

7. Allow the image to dry overnight. Trim the edges, if desired.

TIP

For a stunning variation, transform the black-and-white image into a sepia-toned image (see "Toning" on page 51) before printing.

Apply the gold leaf in a daubing or stippling motion with a foam brush.

Work on a clear clipboard so that you can hold it up to the light to see any areas you may have missed.

Polaroid Image Transfers

I've been making image transfers for about fifteen years now and I'm delighted and somewhat amazed to find that their popularity is still growing. This attests to the fact that the process is much more than a trend, becoming a classic technique in its own right.

A Polaroid image transfer is a simple process of prematurely peeling apart a Polaroid (Type 669), thereby separating the negative from the positive, then transferring the negative onto a non-photographic surface called a receptor sheet. This creates a subtly textured, evocative, and painterly image.

There are lots of variations and variables inherent to this technique, and several books have been published on the subject, but this is my personal favorite tried-and-true recipe.

This image transfer has become my signature piece. All the elements just seemed to fall into place—the lighting, the indirect pose, and the breeze from the fan. Taking it a step further and transforming the original photo into an image transfer enhanced the silhouette effect and added a softness befitting the subject matter.

NOTE

The Polaroid Corporation offers a complete kit and guide to image transfers and other techniques. To find a retailer in your area, call the Polaroid hotline (800-225-1618) or go to www.polaroid.com.

You Will Need

- Polaroid Type 669 film
- One of the following:
  - Vivitar Slide Printer* and a 35mm slide (can be copied from a negative or positive print at a photo lab)
  - Daylab Slide Printer or Daylab Daylight Enlarging System and a 35mm slide
  - Polaroid camera that uses Type 669 film
  - Polaroid Copysystem (uses print instead of slide)
  - Your camera and a detachable Polaroid adaptor back for a live shoot (in which case you don't need a slide)
- 140-pound, hot-pressed, 100-percent rag watercolor paper
- Electric frying pan or means of heating water to 100°F
- Distilled water
- 5 x 7-inch piece of glass (borrow one from a picture frame)
- Squeegee
- Brayer roller
- Scissors or craft knife
- Hair dryer (optional)
  *The Vivitar Slide Printer is no longer being manufactured, but used units can often be found at camera stores and online auction sites such as eBay.

1. Soak a 4 x 5-inch piece of watercolor paper in distilled water heated to 100°F for about two minutes.

2. Place the wet paper on the glass and

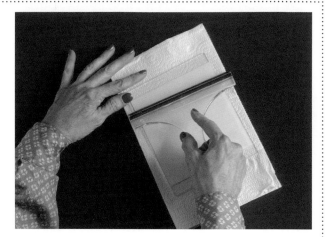

Squeegeeing the watercolor paper will remove excess water.

3. Process the Polaroid according to the initial instructions for the specific piece of equipment you're using. Once you've exposed the image, wait ten to fifteen seconds, then peel apart the film.

Peeling apart the film. If you like, you can cut off part of the tab end to make it easier to separate the positive from the negative.

> ## TIP
> For a neater, cleaner edge, during the ten to fifteen seconds before peeling, cut off the end of the film opposite the pod or tab end with scissors or a craft knife.

4. Place the negative facedown on the watercolor paper and, using the brayer roller, roll six times in one direction with medium pressure.

Transferring the print to the watercolor paper.

5. Keep the negative warm for two minutes using a back-and-forth motion with a hair dryer and/or the palm of your hand.

6. Carefully lift the negative from one corner and gently peel it back, watching to ensure that the gummy emulsion isn't sticking to the print. Depending on how dense the emulsion is, for a subtler effect you might want to rinse the print, rubbing gently to remove some of the color.

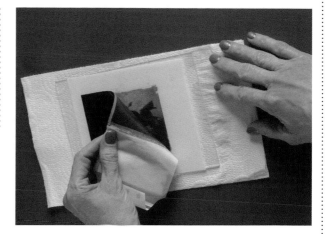

Peeling back the negative reveals the transferred image.

7. Allow the print to dry completely.

8. Scan the image to convert it to a digital file and print as many copies as needed, or use a photocopier.

A Few More Ideas

Working with Polaroid image transfers will undoubtedly inspire your inner artist. It's a wonderful opportunity to experiment with diverse art supplies and materials.

- Use artist pastels, colored pencils, or watercolors to enhance the colors of the transfer.
- For a unique piece of art, transfer the image onto lightly dampened silk instead of paper, stitch it onto a piece of card stock, and frame. (See page 81 for an example of this technique.)
- After prematurely separating the Polaroid, the negative is used to create an image transfer. But don't immediately discard that "positive"—although little dye has had an opportunity to migrate and develop, the washed-out result has a faded beauty of its own.

CHAPTER 4

Sweet Expectations: Pregnancy

Much has been said about the glow of pregnancy, and it's not just a sentimental fallacy. There's something about the biological changes a woman goes through at this magical time in her life that creates an actual sheen. This chapter will give you ideas for capturing the magic in some special photos, which can then be used to create one-of-a-kind shower invitations and other keepsakes.

The Pregnancy Photo Shoot

Not so very long ago—okay, fifty years ago—pregnancy was a private matter. In public, even the word was taboo. Today, I'm happy to report that pregnancy is out and about, and it's beautiful, sensual, and even sexy! Artistically rendered photographs of nude, pregnant celebrities frequently grace the covers of national magazines. Lots of women now flaunt their pregnancy, walking down the street with belly exposed or wearing form-fitting clothing. There are even temporary tattoos designed to focus attention on the expanding belly button itself!

Pregnancy portraiture has become a popular specialty in the world of professional photography, but it's easy to take artistic, professional-quality photos at home. If you're the one that is pregnant, enlist your husband or a sibling or friend who's a shutterbug to take some glamorous photos during your pregnancy. This section will give them some great ideas for capturing you at your most beautiful.

This is the photo that started my interest in pregnancy photography—my daughter, Erin, in 1998.

For the Photographer: Necessities and Niceties to Have on Hand

You have been called upon to capture the emotions and the magic of motherhood in a special keepsake photograph at a cherished time in this woman's life. Celebrate the occasion by making this a day of pampering. Have plenty of bottled water on hand, maybe even crackers and cheese or cookies and some juice or herbal tea. Provide a comfortable area for the mother-to-be to relax between setups.

Grainy black-and-white film, draped fabric, dramatic lighting, and an indirect gaze contribute to the fine-art quality of this image.

What-to-Expect Session Tips for the Expectant Mom

HERE ARE SOME TIPS FOR MAKING THE MOST OF THE PHOTO SESSION.

- Schedule your session to take place six to ten weeks before your due date.
- Eat a light snack before the shoot.
- Don't wear anything with elastic (even undergarments) that may create marks on your skin.
- Bring any favorite articles of clothing—your husband's dress shirt or a simple piece of black or white lingerie—although fabric for draping should be provided.
- Don't wear makeup that contains glitter.
- Bring bottled water.
- Bring a favorite music CD that will help you to feel relaxed.
- Be prepared to look and feel like the goddess you are!

Styling the Session

Rather than beginning with a preconceived idea of the portrait you're about to shoot, find out what the mom-to-be has in mind. Does she lean toward black-and-white or color shots, romantic or straightforward?

You'll also want to discover your subject's comfort level in exposing her own pregnancy. How much skin does she want to reveal? The wardrobe she has brought will tell you a lot. Is it mostly lingerie, sweats, or tailored and fitted maternity clothing?

In this studio setup, color reigns supreme. A low red chair and a red seamless backdrop provide a striking accent to the simple black-and-white outfit. Alison is clearly relaxed and enjoying herself—it's her day to feel pampered and beautiful.

Attire

Clothing can obscure the natural beauty of the rounded body. As an alternative, have yards of silky or gauzy fabric on hand: It can be wrapped and draped to cover where needed, expose where desired, and help to evoke a timeless quality perfectly suited to the occasion.

My experience has been that most pregnant women are comfortable starting their session dressed in comfortable clothing, then switching to draped fabric, and eventually dropping everything and allowing me to shoot some tasteful nudes, or at least partial nudes. I think women are secretly enchanted by the changes their bodies are going through, and, not surprisingly, so are their mates. That's why they've sought to capture this period in their lives on film.

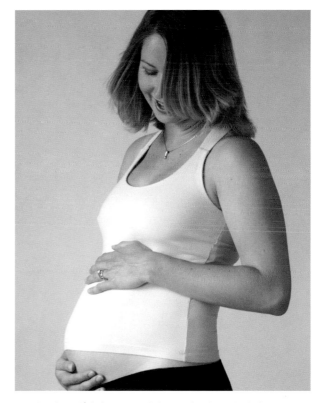

A modern classic. Today's maternity clothes are often designed to be form fitting and to expose the belly. Posing Nicole against a simple seamless background helps to focus attention on the subject at hand.

Setting the Mood

I like to add to the ambience of the session by having some classical music or jazz playing in the background. If the expectant mom seems nervous in front of the camera, I try to establish a relaxing tone by asking her if she knows the gender of the baby, if she has any other children, or if she's chosen the baby's name. These types of questions invariably lead to lighthearted, lively discussion. If she seems self-conscious about stretch marks or her *linea nigra* (the dark line that appears vertically on the abdomen during pregnancy), assure her that you will be providing props and/or fabric to camouflage that area or, if you're adept at doing so, "fixing it in Photoshop."

A man's button-down shirt offers lots of possibilities, whether with one or two buttons fastened or hanging open to cast strategic shadows, and adds a wonderful complement to the feminine content of the photograph.

Some strategic burning and dodging in Photoshop and a stylized high key treatment preserve Danielle's modesty.

*This is now a photo she just **might** feel comfortable showing her grandmother.*

Setting Up the Pose

As this is a pregnancy portrait, you'll want to emphasize the belly. I have to laugh when I remember the young woman who came to me when she was six months along exclaiming, "I'm so huge!" We shot some photos, but I took a chance and asked her to come back in two months to complete the session. When she compared the proofs from this session to the earlier one, she was amazed: You could barely tell she was pregnant at six months!

As you position your subject, notice the rounded shapes and curved lines of the pregnant form and use lighting to accentuate them, be it natural, room lighting, or strobe. Soft natural light can provide just the right amount and quality of illumination. In any event, it's usually preferable not to shoot straight on with the light source even with the camera axis: The curves and shadows will be lost, making the image confusing.

For a definitive silhouette effect, drape a sheet or a length of lightweight white fabric over a large window or a door and have the expectant mother stand in front of it, turning to the side. This will emphasize the graceful curve of the belly and help to minimize other areas that might be a source of self-consciousness. To add to the mood of the image, place a fan nearby to softly ruffle hair and/or fabric.

As with any portrait, keep the background free from clutter. Sometimes a prop such as a flower or stuffed animal adds emotional content to the shot, as long as it's not visually distracting; it also gives the subject something to do with her hands. A simple facial gesture such as a downward or upward gaze adds subtext of

peaceful reverie; a radiant smile tells something of the amazing journey she is on, filled with joy and anticipation.

The mom-to-be might also want to include the father and older children in the photo session. Any photos that result would be instant family keepsakes.

A stuffed teddy bear is a perfectly sweet prop.

Ask other family members to join in to add to the richness of the portrait. Loving looks, gentle hand gestures, and playfulness all add to the story told in celebration of family.

Location

All that's required is a good-sized room with lots of natural light and a minimum amount of clutter to set up a "studio." Digital cameras and fast film allow you to work with ISO settings that will accommodate almost any light, so there's really no need for cumbersome lighting equipment unless you really want it. And, believe it or not, a garage also makes an ideal studio. Have your subject stand near the garage door opening; the light spilling in off the driveway will provide the perfect glow and just the right amount of shadow fall-off. Just in case, be sure to bring some fabric and clamps or clothespins to hang a makeshift backdrop to hide the garage "décor" or clutter.

Shooting outdoors is another appealing option. Natural settings such as the beach, a field, or a garden provide artistic backgrounds with a timeless quality to complement a photograph that celebrates the eternal feminine mystique. The weather and time of day will contribute to the overall tone of the session, be it a bright sunny day, at sunset, or on a cloudy day.

This unusual shot was not planned. Inspiration struck as Amanda began walking among the pilings under the pier. The semi-darkness necessitated an ISO of 800, which created lots of digital "noise."

Stock Photography

Advertising agencies, Web designers, graphic designers, and lots of other entities frequently take advantage of stock photography—images that aren't taken for a specific client or purpose but are used and reused for multiple assignments. You can take your own stock images—rubber duckies, baby shoes, stuffed teddy bears, and the like—which you can incorporate into your projects. Taking stock shots is fun; you have complete control and can get really creative, and you can also transform them into image transfers or manipulate them in Photoshop. Say you're designing a baby shower invitation and the mother-to-be is camera shy; a stock image may be the perfect solution. After all, not every woman wants a photo of her pregnant self on the cover of her baby shower invitation.

These baby-themed stationery pieces feature Polaroid image transfers (see page 64 for step-by-step instructions). For the baby shoes cards,
I made two image transfers using the same 35mm slide, then added watercolor paints to create "boy" and "girl" versions.
The "painting" could just as easily—or even more easily—be accomplished in Photoshop.

Simply Elegant Baby Shower Invitation

The photo session of the mother-to-be is bound to produce a magnificent image guaranteed to elicit oohs and aahs. What better way to showcase it than on a baby shower invitation! Here are instructions for creating a simple, elegant invitation, laid out in Photoshop and designed to make the most of that image. This layout produces two top-folding invitations. To add a personal touch, the invitation details—guest of honor, date, time, place, etc.—can be filled in by hand.

You Will Need

- A photo from the pregnancy photo session
- Heavyweight textured digital photo paper (8 1/2 x 11 inches) (e.g., Hahnemuhle Photo Rag Duo or Arches Infinity [Textured])
- Bone folder (for scoring and smoothing)
- Matte photo paper (8 1/2 x 11 inches)
- Complementary card stock (optional)
- Glue stick
- Craft glue
- Scotch 3M double-sided foam tape
- Paper cutter or craft knife
- Ruler
- Self-healing cutting mat
- Envelopes (4 3/8 x 5 3/4 inches)
- Baby's breath or similar type of dried or paper flowers

For this charming invitation, the original photograph was transformed into a painterly Polaroid image transfer (see page 63) and is complemented by a simple yet feminine treatment

1. Choose File>New and select the Letter Preset option. As a rule of thumb, RGB Color mode and 300 ppi resolution are suitable for all of the projects detailed in this book. Make sure Rulers is checked in the View menu. From the Rulers, drag out a vertical Guide at 4 1/4 inches and a horizontal Guide at 5 1/2 inches as shown to delineate the invitation dimensions and to assist in layout. (Guides will not appear on printed piece.) Save the new file but don't close it.

Here, Guides are used to visually divide the layout into four equal quadrants.

TIP
Save the file as a template (e.g., Top-Fold Template) so that in the future you can use it as the basis for other top-folding cards and invitations.

2. For an invitation that is to be filled in by hand, you'll want to draw some lines. First, add a couple more Guides to help align the starting and ending points of each line. Then, select the Brush tool (B) with a small diameter (e.g., 2 or 3 pixels) and, in the bottom left quadrant of the layout, hold down the Shift key and draw the first line. Using the vertical Ruler to judge the distance from one line to the next, draw as many more lines as you wish. If you prefer, you can use the Type tool (T) to lay out the invitation text itself instead of leaving it to be filled in by hand. I added the words "You're Invited" at the top.

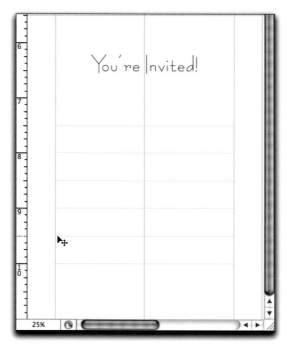

Use the vertical Ruler to judge the distance from one line to the next. (Font: Bernard Fashion ICG)

3. In the Layers palette, select the visible layers and, holding down the Option/Alt key and the Shift key, click and drag a copy over to the right lower quadrant.

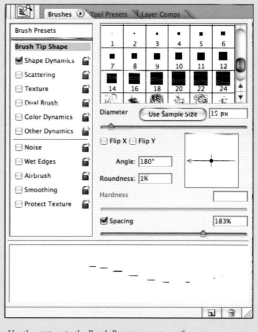

Duplicating the layout in the bottom-right quadrant allows you to print two invitations at once.

4. Print the layout on the heavy weight textured paper.

5. Cut the sheet in half to create two 4 1/4 x 11-inch cards. Using a bone folder to create a sharp fold (see page 20), fold each card in half crosswise so that the image can be affixed to the cover.

6. Open an image in Photoshop and go to Image>Image Size to reduce its size to about 1 1/4 x 1 3/4 inches at 300 ppi. Go to Select>All, then Edit>Copy.

7. In Photoshop, open a *new* letter-size file and drag out Guides to divide the sheet into twenty-five equal segments. Be sure to leave a margin on all four sides of the page—most printers don't print to the edges. Now go to Edit>Paste and paste the same number of copies of the image, moving each one into its own segment. (Abutting the Guides helps to align them; remember, the Guides won't show when printed.)
   Print onto a sheet of matte photo paper using photo-quality printer settings.

Sign on the Dotted Line

Prefer broken lines? Here's a great feature in Photoshop few people seem to know about: First, click on the Brush tool (B). Under the Window menu, click on Brushes to open the Brush Preset menu. Click on the little right-facing triangle next to the word "Brush" and choose Expanded View. Click on the triangle again and choose Square Brushes, then opt to append the Square Brushes to your brush palette. Scroll to display the square brushes and click on one, any one. Click on the words "Brush Tip Shape" at the top of the Brush Preset menu). Set Diameter to 15 pixels, Angle to 180°, Roundness to 1 percent and adjust the Spacing to something well over 100, say 150. In your open file, hold down the Shift key to draw a straight horizontal broken line. If necessary, go back and adjust the diameter and/or spacing settings to your liking.

Use the options in the Brush Presets menu to easily create customized dotted lines in your layouts.

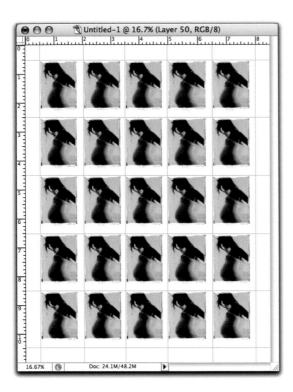

You can print about twenty-five 1 1/4 x 1 3/4-inch images on one 8 1/2 x 11-inch piece of paper.

8. Trim each reproduction to size, including a small border if desired.

9. Cut a piece of the same heavyweight paper or complementary card stock to about 1/2 inch larger overall than the trimmed reproduction. Center and use a glue stick to adhere the image onto the piece of card stock, then affix a piece of double-sided foam tape to the back of the image assembly, remove the protective strip, and mount it onto the front of the folded card. Repeat for the remaining reproductions.

10. Affix a sprig of baby's breath or other embellishment using craft glue.

Baby Shower Invitation Etiquette

Of course, you want your shower invitations to be aesthetically pleasing, but remember that they are first and foremost meant to convey information. Here are a few tips to make sure you don't forget anything:

- Invitations should be sent out four to six weeks before the event.
- Be sure to include gift registry information if applicable.
- Always include the name of the hostess so that people know who they are calling when they RSVP.
- In our increasingly informal society, an etiquette problem has cropped up: Invited guests often "forget" to RSVP. A simple solution is to substitute "Regrets Only" for RSVP.

A Few More Ideas

- Add decorative paper, ribbon, cord, or raffia.
- Hang charms (available at craft stores) from a piece of decorative string or thin cord strung across the top of the invitation.
- To create invitations with the images printed directly on them, choose a double-sided paper, follow steps 1 through 3, and print the layout.

Click the eye icon next to the layers for the lines and/or type to turn them off. Insert the images in the same quadrants, then reinsert the paper in the printer by both flipping it over and rotating it. Print the layout again. Cut the sheet in half and fold as described in step 5.

This variation features a Polaroid image (see page 45) transferred onto silk and then stitched to paper. Each card is an original piece of art.

Classic Side-Fold Invitation

The side-fold or book-style card is a versatile, traditional format similar to a greeting card. An appropriate "teaser" line is often printed on the cover, with the event information printed on the inside. Follow these step-by-step instructions to create two $4\,1/4$ x $5\,1/2$-inch folded baby shower invitations out of one letter-size sheet of paper. Each invitation will fit into a standard envelope measuring $4\,3/8$ x $5\,3/4$ inches.

You Will Need
- A photo from the pregnancy photo session
- Double-sided fine art–quality digital paper ($8\,1/2$ x 11 inches)
- Paper cutter or craft knife
- Ruler
- Self-healing cutting mat
- Bone folder
- Envelopes ($4\,3/8$ x $5\,3/4$ inches)

1. Choose File>New and select the Letter Preset option. The mode should be RGB Color and the resolution 300 ppi. From the Ruler, drag out a vertical Guide at $4\,1/4$ inches and a horizontal Guide at $5\,1/2$ inches to delineate the invitation dimensions and to assist in layout. (Guides will not appear on printed piece.) Save the new file but don't close it.

2. Now open the file containing the photograph you would like to incorporate in the layout. If the file contains layers, flatten the image. Make sure the resolution is 300 ppi. Crop and/or resize the image as desired for placement within the front cover of the invitation. Go to Select>All, then Edit>Copy. Close the *original* image file *without saving it.*

3. Return to the open file by clicking on the window. Go to Edit>Paste. Use the Move tool (V) to drag the image into position within the upper-right quadrant of the layout as shown. Repeat Edit>Paste and move the second image into position in the lower layout. Use the Rulers and drag out additional Guides as needed to help align the images within the layouts.

The dramatic image for this invitation was chosen to complement the setting of the baby shower—lunch and art at the Getty Museum in Los Angeles. (Fonts: Caslon Book and Liana)

Hints for Working with Text

- Depending on the size of the type, it's sometimes difficult to move text with the Move tool. If you can't "grab" the text to drag it, use the arrow keys to move it into position.
- The Type tool is a little possessive—sometimes it just won't let go. Click on another tool to disengage it.
- To edit text at any time, double-click on the T thumbnail in the Layers palette to select (highlight) the type and choose another font and/or size.

TIP

To resize the image, with the image layer highlighted in the Layers palette, go to Edit>Transform>Scale. In the Options bar, change the percentages in the height and width boxes (e.g., 50 percent). Press Return/Enter to apply the transformation.

4. To add cover text, click on the Type tool (T) and then click on the upper-right quadrant. Choose a font style and size and then type the text. Click on the Move tool and use the arrow keys to position the text precisely where you want it.

5. In the Layers palette, select the visible layers and, holding down the Option/Alt key and the Shift key, click and drag a copy into the lower layout.

6. To add type, such as the name of the designer of the piece (i.e., you!) on the back (in the example, I included my studio contact information), click on the Type tool, choose a font style and size, and type within the upper-left quadrant of the layout. Click on the Move tool and use the arrow keys to move the info into precise position. Go to Layer>Duplicate Layer, click OK, and move the second layer of text into place in the lower layout.

The layout, showing the front and back covers of the invitation.

7. To add interior text, in the Layers palette, click the eye icons next to the existing image and text layers to render them temporarily invisible. Lay out the inside text for one invitation in the upper-right quadrant. Go to Layer>Duplicate Layer, click OK, and then use the Move tool and/or the arrow keys to move the text into position in the lower layout.

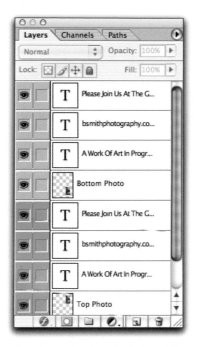

The layout of the interior of the invitation.

Renaming and/or color coding the layers in Layers palette will help you remember which is which.

8. At this point you'll have several layers. To avoid confusion, you might want to name them. In the Layers palette, highlighting each layer in turn, double-click on the layer designation, and type in a description. Or color code the layers, say, differentiating the cover layers from the inside text layers or the upper layout from the lower layout. To do this, again in the Layers palette, highlight each layer in turn, go to Layer>Layer Properties, and select a color.

9. To print the cover: With only the cover layers activated in the Layers palette, print one sheet using the best photo printer settings.

10. To print the inside text: Turn off the cover layers and activate the inside text layers. Turn your paper over (but don't rotate it!), and print the second side.

11. Use a paper cutter or craft knife to cut the sheet in half, creating two cards.

12. Fold each card in half and then cover the fold with a piece of scrap paper and burnish with the broad edge of a bone folder to flatten smoothly. (For heavier card stock, use the pointed end of the bone folder to score a fold line before folding.)

TIP

Depending on your printer, you may have to nudge the image or text layers a bit so that everything lines up perfectly. That's the beauty of layers, and that's also why it's imperative to always test print on inexpensive paper first! If you make any changes, be sure to save the tweaked version.

Layered Invitation

....

Transparency film sheets manufactured by 3M (which are also used in making Auratones) open up a world of creative possibilities as demonstrated in this project. Once you have created a file with each graphic element on a separate layer, you can create interesting dimensional effects by printing on two or more layers of transparency film. Alternatively, simply layer an image printed on transparency film over text printed on paper for a pleasing visual and tactile quality, or vice-versa—print the text on the film to overlay an image. Leave the layers loose, or unite them with a brad or eyelet.

You Will Need

- One or more photos
- 3M Multipurpose Transparency Film
- Paper cutter, scissors, or craft knife
- Ruler
- Self-healing cutting mat
- White paper
- Eyelet, brad, or clip (optional)
- Envelopes

1. Choose File>New and create a custom size of 5 x 5 inches. (This size enables you to print two layers out of one letter-size sheet of transparency film, so in Page Layout, the Paper Size will be letter.) The mode should be RGB Color and the resolution 300 ppi. Save the new file but don't close it.

2. Open the files containing the photographs you would like to incorporate in the layout. You might choose a textural background from your stock photo file (see page 58) and a portrait. Crop and/or resize the images as desired for placement within the layout. Make sure the resolution for each file is 300 ppi.

3. Copy and paste or click and drag each file into the new file you opened in step 1. Note that each image is on its own layer in the Layers palette. Close the image files without saving them.

Layers of transparencies make a fun "interactive" invitation. Each layer is printed with a different element (e.g., background, text, image), and when stacked you see a single, united layout. (Fonts: P22 Cezanne and Interludee)

4. Add a new layer (or multiple layers) and type the text.

5. Now take the time to finesse the layout. If necessary, with the appropriate layer highlighted in the Layers palette, go to Select>All, then Edit>Transform>Scale and resize the images as needed. (Remember to hold down the Shift key to maintain the height-to-width ratio.) Add layer masks for increased control and flexibility (see steps 4–6 on page 58.) Edit the text layer(s) using the features in the Character palette.

6. Okay, here's the tricky part: You'll be printing on the rough side of the transparency film, even though ultimately the smooth side will face up. This means you need to flip the contents of each layer horizontally before printing so that it appears in its proper orientation once the sheet is turned over. So in succession, in the Layers palette, highlight one layer, go to Edit>Transform>Flip Horizontal, then print that layer onto a transparency sheet. Follow the same procedure with the other layers. If you have text on more than one layer, you'll probably want to merge those layers or select them as one unit before printing.

7. Trim each sheet to size. Place a piece of white paper behind the bottom layer, then stack and unite the layers with an eyelet or clip, or leave them loose so that they can be rearranged "interactively." My favorite way of presenting them is loose in a nesting-type envelope (see opposite below): Just fold the flaps in and seal with a decorative label.

Below and opposite, you can see each layer of the invitation activated individually, so that the layers can be printed on separate sheets.

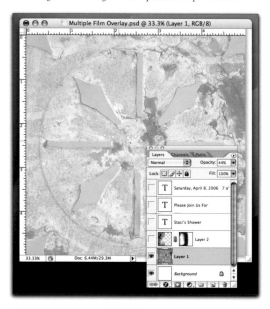

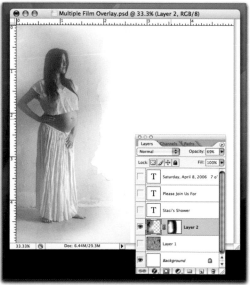

Nesting envelope template.

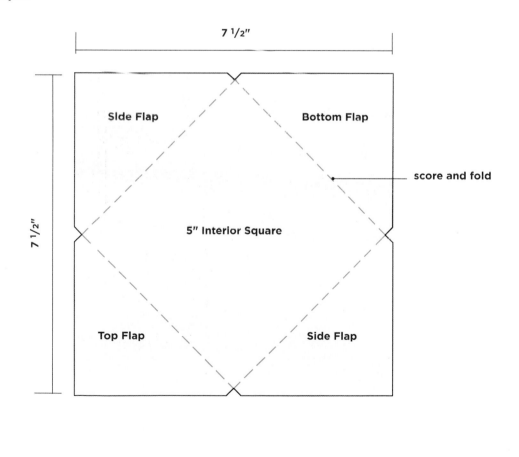

CHAPTER 5

Celebrating the Mom-to-Be: The Baby Shower

The baby shower is a wonderful opportunity to capture photos of the expectant mom and her loved ones relaxed and enjoying themselves, images she'll certainly want to preserve in unique photo-based albums and thank-you notes. Handmade favors that feature photos from the pregnancy session are also sure to be a big hit!

Capturing the Fun with Great Photos

A baby shower is a celebration of the arrival of a new member of the family, and as such it deserves to be beautifully and well documented. Approach this event with the intention of using your camera to tell the story of the event as it unfolds.

You don't need to bring anything other than your camera and perhaps a tripod, if you'll be shooting indoors in low light. For the most part, shoot from the periphery to capture great snapshots with a photojournalistic quality, although some casual poses are a must. I'm in the habit of carrying two cameras to every event, and for showers, one is almost always a Polaroid. The meeting-and-greeting portion of the event is the perfect opportunity to take an instant photo of each guest that is then inserted directly into the guest book as the day progresses. Guests can sign the page featuring their photo at any time during the day, adding personal thoughts and messages.

Some casual, friendly poses capture the feeling of the day and will add to the warmth of the album.

Guest books filled with Polaroids and special thoughts are the perfect accompaniment to a storybook photo album filled with the rest of the images taken throughout the day.

A Big Idea

If there are beautiful photos of the mom-to-be from a pregnancy photo session, consider enlarging them and matting or mounting them—or even making them into posters at a quick print shop—and displaying them at the baby shower. The guest of honor will be proud, and guests will be pleased to have the opportunity to see the photos.

Scene Setters

Arrive early to grab some "scene setters"—still life shots of the decorations, table settings, and guest book at the ready—to commemorate the caring thought and attention to detail that went into the planning of this special event. You'll want to evoke a sense of time and place, whether it's a garden brunch, lunch at someone's home, a late afternoon high tea at an elegant restaurant, or an unusual event such as a picnic or an afternoon of art at a museum or gallery. In this way, the album you ultimately create featuring those images within its pages becomes, in essence, a storybook.

The hostess went all out in decorating for her special friend's baby shower. The "cake" centerpiece was actually made out of disposable diapers. Preserving thoughtful details like this is a must.

In the pink. A shallow depth of field (f /4.5) throws the background out of focus, but it's clear this shower celebrates the impending arrival of a baby girl. Don't forget to save some of the wrappings to decorate the baby shower album (see page 101).

Activities

Most showers follow a fairly predictable time-table: meeting and greeting, activities, food and drink (usually including a special cake or other dessert), and finally the opening of gifts, although some guests of honor prefer to open their gifts later in the privacy of their own home.

Many showers include party games and contests—matching baby pictures to guests, writing down song titles containing the word *baby*, word scrambles, and guessing at the girth of the mother-to-be. A photojournalistic approach to these types of activities will un-doubtedly result in some very humorous shots.

The partaking of food and drink is another highlight of the event, although it's for the most part best left unphotographed—*nobody* looks good in the act of chewing! Take some "table shots"—group photos of the guests at each table—either immediately before the food is served or after. Be sure to get a close-up of the cake or other dessert.

If gifts are opened on site, photo ops abound: the person in charge of collecting bits of ribbon for a memento, someone else writing down the details of who gave what, and, of course, the "ooh!' and "aah!" reactions of the guest of honor as well as the guests as tiny apparel and other gorgeous gifts are unwrapped.

Be sure to take plenty of photos of the guest of honor interacting with her friends and family members and try to stay until the very end to capture the warm hugs and goodbyes.

Reaction shots add an element of genuine emotion to the record of the day.

Showers often include games and activities. On this occasion guests were invited to decorate "onesies."

Table shots are standard fare at most event, but it's best to get them before the food has been served so that the settings are still fresh and no one is caught with her mouth full.

Spiral-Bound Guest Book

Before the shower, create a guest book for the baby shower that incorporates a photo of the expectant mom. You can also preserve a copy of the invitation on the first page. During the shower, Polaroids may be taken and inserted, and guests can write their personal thoughts and best wishes. You can also wait until after the shower to decorate the guest book, taking it with you when you leave and then sending it to the guest of honor when it's complete.

You Will Need

- **A plain spiral-bound album***
- **For front cover with die-cut window (Method 1 below):**
  - Ellison die cutter and die
  - One sheet of decorative paper, 1 inch taller and $1/2$ inch wider than the cover, excluding the spine (hole) area
- **For front cover with manually cut window (Method 2 below):**
  - One piece of lightweight card stock, $1/4$ inch smaller in length and width than the cover, excluding the spine (hole) area
  - One sheet of decorative paper, 1 inch larger in length and width than the card stock
- **For the back cover: One sheet of decorative paper, 1 inch taller and $1/2$ inch wider than the cover excluding the spine (hole) area**

- **For the cover endpapers: Two sheets of complementary paper, or paper remnants from gifts, cut slightly smaller than the covers**
- **A photo**
- **Spray adhesive**
- **Craft glue**
- **Bone folder**
- **Tape**
- **Craft knife**
- **Ruler**
- **Self-healing cutting mat**
- **Complementary paper to cover spine (optional)**
- **Envelope to hold mementos (optional)**
- **Skeleton leaves and/or millinery flower for decoration (optional)**
  *Both Canson and Cachet albums use a spiral system that makes removing and replacing covers and pages easy.

A spiral-bound guest book becomes a charming keepsake filled with Polaroid snapshots, handwritten messages, and mementos. A larger coordinating album becomes a scrapbook chronicling the storybook aspect of the event with more photos as well as a list of gifts received and the shower cards inserted in a special envelope. Japanese momi *paper ties the two together.*

Guests

_____
_____
_____
_____
_____
_____

You might want to remove a few of the pages, print the word Guests *and signature lines on them, and then reinsert them into the album.*

(Font: Bickley Script)

TIP

To customize an album or guestbook, print a placard on heavyweight paper. Cut it out and adhere it securely to the front of the cover. You can create a layered placard by first wrapping a piece of card stock with decorative paper, attaching the printed card to it, then adhering the assembly to the cover.

Creating the Covers: Method 1

This method involves the use of an Ellison die cutter—a kind of giant paper punch, and the only tabletop tool I know of that enables you to cut precise sizeable shapes out of a wide range of paper stock, from lightweight paper to heavyweight card or matboard.

1. Carefully remove the covers from the spiral album, being careful not to bend the coil out of shape. Use an Ellison die cutter to punch out a window in the front cover (see page 17).

2. Apply a mist of spray adhesive to a sheet of decorative paper and, sticky side down, center it over the front cover at the top and bottom, covering the window but not the holes along the spine edge. It's easiest to accomplish this by lining up the edge of the sheet along the holes first and then pressing in a fanning motion to smooth it and remove any air bubbles.

Lining up the decorative paper against the cover holes

3. Turn the assembly over and fold in each outside corner at a squared diagonal, then fold the top flap down, the side flap in, and the bottom flap up. Use the bone folder to make sure all corners and edges are very snug.

Folding in an outside corner at a squared diagonal for a crisp corner.

4. With the front cover facing down, use a craft knife to cut an X in the window from corner to corner. Bring the flaps through to the inside, trim off the points, and press the flaps down. Use your fingers or the edge of the bone folder to ensure a neat, snug adhesion around the edges of the window.

Wrapping the paper flaps around the edges of the window creates a finished look.

5. Cover the back cover with decorative paper, but do not make a window.

6. Tape the photo to the back of the front cover so that it is aligned properly within the window.

Creating the Covers: Method 2

As an alternative to a die-cut window, use a craft knife to cut a window in a lightweight piece of cardboard, wrap it with decorative paper, and adhere it to the cover of an album.

A simple collage of skeleton leaves and a tiny millinery flower add the perfect feminine accent to this album cover.

1. Carefully remove the covers from the spiral album. Cut a piece of plain paper to the size of the desired window for use as a template and glue it in place where you would like the window to be on the lightweight card stock. Use a craft knife and ruler to cut out the window.

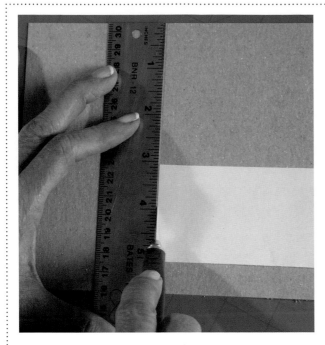

Cutting a window in the card stock with a craft knife

2. Apply a mist of spray adhesive to the front side of the card stock and center it on the complementary paper, sticky side down, covering the window. Press in a fanning motion to smooth and remove any air bubbles.

3. Fold in each outside corner at a squared diagonal and then fold the top flap down, the side flaps in, and the bottom flap up.

4. Turn the assembly over and, using a craft knife, cut an X in the window from corner to corner. Bring the flaps through to the inside, trim off the points if they extend beyond the edges, and glue or tape the flaps down.

5. Tape a photo into position to show through the window. Now adhere the entire assembly to the album cover itself.

Final Steps

A few final details add to the warmth of the personal touch.

1. Adhere the endpapers to the inside of both the front and back covers and smooth with the bone folder.

2. Adhere an envelope to the inside of the back cover for storing a CD—with a custom label, of course (see page 129)—containing the images shot during the shower. Press covers with heavy books overnight to prevent wrinkles or warping.

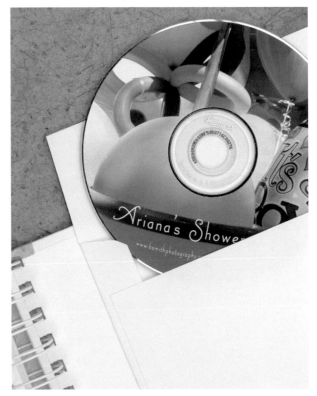

Envelopes are handy additions to the inside covers; use double-sided tape to attach them. Add pretty vellum envelopes to the pages within the album to create pockets for holding miscellaneous mementos such as cards and game paraphernalia.

TIP

I often scrounge through the discarded wrappings at a shower looking for items I can later use to decorate the guest book or album. Pretty papers, ribbons, gift tags, cards, even charms and other three-dimensional objects are perfect for mixed media collage to line the inside covers.

Covering the Spiral (Optional)

At this point, photos can now be inserted in the album using photo corners or double-sided photo mounts. Extra pages may be removed. Or take it a step further by covering the spiral. If you choose to cover the spiral spine, a malleable yet strong decorative paper like Japanese *momi* paper is perfect; its crinkly texture makes it very forgiving, and its leather-like texture helps to protect the album from wear and tear.

1. With the covers already attached to the album, measure 1 1/2 inches in from the spine edge on the right side of both the front and back covers and mark with pencil as a gluing guideline.

2. Cut the chosen piece of decorative paper equal to the height of the covers plus 1/2 inch and wide enough to cover the spiral, at least 1 1/2 inches of the spine edge of both the front and back covers, plus 1/2 inch. (About 7 inches total width is usually sufficient.)

3. Turn in all corners and edges 1/4 inch. Make sure that the paper is exactly the height of the album covers.

4. Apply craft glue to the spine area of the front cover up to the gluing guideline but not including the 1/4-inch border area containing the holes.

5. Adhere the decorative paper to the front cover, just covering the pencil line.

6. Apply craft glue to the spine area of the back cover up to the gluing guideline but not including the 1/4-inch border containing the holes.

7. Make sure the prongs of the spiral coil are nestled within the coil at the back of the album. Now draw the paper from the front cover over the spiral and adhere it to the back cover as well, just covering the pencil line. Be sure all edges are perfectly aligned and that the spine is snugly covered.

Create a mixed-media collage to line the inside covers using memorabilia from the shower—the invitation, photos, swatches of wrapping paper, cards, ribbon, etc.

Photo Soap Favors

These soaps are so special that in all likelihood they'll be kept as keepsakes and never actually used. If you do want to make them "waterproof," simply laminate the photo or apply a coat of spray adhesive to a separate layer of acetate and adhere it to the printed side of the image before inserting into the mold. This will prevent the ink from running once water reaches it.

What more apt favor for a shower than soap? Molds are available in a variety of shapes and sizes.

You Will Need

- A photo
- 3M Inkjet Transparency Film
- Inkjet printer
- Clear glycerin soap (looks almost opaque in package)
- A microwave oven or double boiler
- A mold (available at craft stores and online)
- Scissors or craft knife
- Clear plastic wrap
- Raffia, ribbon, or cord
- Labels (optional)

1. Open a photo file and resize. The image should be slightly smaller than the mold. Before printing, flip the image horizontally in Photoshop (Image>Rotate Canvas>Flip Canvas Horizontal); it will appear in its proper orientation when the sheet is turned face up. Print photo on transparency film and trim.

2. Heat a sufficient amount of glycerin soap in the microwave on High for about one minute or in a double boiler until melted.

3. Pour the soap to fill the mold halfway. Wait about twenty minutes to allow a "skin" to form, then carefully place the photograph over the skin and pour in more melted soap to fill the mold. If the photo floats up, push it down with the tip of a pin or other small object and hold it there for a moment as the soap begins to set.

TIP

For a craftier look, cut off the bottom 2 inches of a milk carton and use that as a mold.

4. Allow the soap to set for several hours or for one hour in the refrigerator. Do not put it in the freezer.

5. Apply pressure over different areas to release the soap from the mold.

6. Use a sharp knife to clean up the edges.

7. Wrap individual bars in clear plastic wrap, then seal with a round label. Add raffia, ribbon, or cord. Optionally, seal with a decorative label or one printed with the name of the guest of honor and the date, or attach a gift tag (see page 150).

Troubleshooting Tips

Slight imperfections are part of the charm of handcrafted gifts, so don't fret over a little cloud or bubble here and there. Of course, practice does make perfect.

- Use a wire whisk or fork to gently stir the melted soap to remove the majority of bubbles and to minimize cloudiness.
- Use a kitchen utensil or chopstick to skim off any undissolved soap that rises to the top.
- Avoid handling the soap to minimize fingerprints; if they do appear, rinse them off and let the soap dry undisturbed.

Cartes Postales
Thank-you Notes

This baby shower was held in a charming French restaurant, so a faux French postcard was the perfect thank-you note. Taking individual table shots meant that the guests seated at each table could be featured on their own *"carte postale"*.

Once you've created a postcard template, you can use it again and again for a multitude of purposes, adapting it to suit your needs. I created an African version I use to complement photos I took in Kenya, changing "Merci" to "Jambo!" which means "Hello!" in Swahili. I also have a Hawaiian version that says "Aloha" and one that says "Mahalo!," which means "Thank you!".

You Will Need

- **A photo or photos from the baby shower**
- **Double-sided matte photo paper**
- **Paper cutter**
- **Corner punch (optional)**

1. In Photoshop, choose File>New and create a custom-sized document of 4 1/4 x 6 inches (300 ppi).

2. (Opt.) Open a file containing a background or download one of mine—the background used in the sample is "Old Paper," which was made by scanning the discolored back of an old photograph. If necessary, go to Image>Image Size and crop and/or resize your background image to 4 1/4 x 6 inches (300 ppi), then copy and paste or click and drag it into the open file, and close the original file without saving it.

TIP

Create your own template from scratch or feel free to download mine at www.bsmithphotography.com/goodies, where you'll also find some cool borders and backgrounds.

The front image on this "carte postale" was enhanced in Photoshop with the "Monday Morning" Nik

filter. The back of the card incorporates a scanned textured background layer to add to its vintage look.

(Fonts: Bodoni Classic Deco and P22 Cezanne)

3. Select the Type tool (T) and add the text elements, each on a separate layer so that you can move them around and edit them individually. Use a couple of different fonts. Center a line of vertical text containing image details. To create vertical text, type as usual, then go to Edit>Transform>Rotate 90° CW (clockwise).

   To create the address lines, hold down the Shift key as you draw with a small (e.g., 2 pixel) Brush. Use the Rulers and Guides to help with alignment. (For a more detailed explanation, refer to page 78.)

4. (Opt.) To create a stamp box, see page 79 for instructions on how to create broken or dotted lines. (I used Bodoni for the type in the stamp box.)

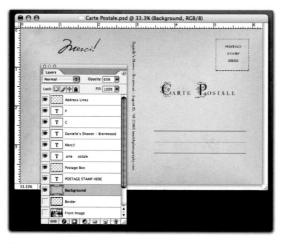

Here you can see the multiple layers contained in this file. The active layers—with the "eye" icons to their left—constitute the back of the postcard (shown); the inactive layers (without eyes) are for the front of the postcard.

5. Now open an image file and, if necessary, resize or crop it to 4 1/4 x 6 inches (300 ppi), then copy and paste or click and drag it into the open file. Close the original file without saving it.

6. (Opt.) Add a border (or download one of mine). (See "Adding Borders" on page 52.)

7. At this point, you could print one side of the postcard on a sheet of paper with only the relevant layers activated, then deactivate those layers and activate the remaining layers, turn the sheet over, and print the reverse side. But to maximize efficiency in terms of time and materials, why not print two postcards on one sheet? Here's how:

   Open a new letter-size file (300 ppi). Drag out Guides 1 inch from the top of the window and 1 inch from the bottom.

8. Click on the postcard file window. Activate the cover layers by clicking on the eye icons for those layers in the Layers palette. Make sure none of the reverse-side layers is visible in the window. Flatten the layers (Layer>Flatten Image), but *do not* save the file, then copy and paste or hold down the Shift key and click and drag into the new letter-size file. Repeat to add a second layout.

TIP

If you're uneasy about temporarily flattening the layers because you think you might forget and save the flattened file, thus losing all your layers, first go to Image>Duplicate, save and close the original layered file, and use the duplicate version for flattening.

Printing two postcards on one sheet of paper saves time and money.

10. Go back to the original postcard file, go to Edit>Undo to cancel the last step (flatten), deactivate the front layers, activate the reverse-side layers, flatten the layers, then copy and paste or hold down the Shift key and click and drag into the letter size sheet as before, aligning the back layers with the front layers. You now have four layers in the Layers palette.

TIP

If your postcard layout has a white background, it will help to add a stroke to each layout for use as a trim guide. With each layer in turn activated, go to Edit>Stroke and choose a 2-pixel black stroke and the center location. Be sure to trim so that the stroke is discarded.

9. Note that there are now two new layers in the Layers palette. Each one is centered both horizontally and vertically within the window, so it looks like there's just one image. Choose the Move tool (V) and, holding down the Shift key, move one layer into position against the top Guide. Then hold down the Shift key and move the second layer into position against the bottom Guide. (Holding down the Shift key keeps them in perfect vertical alignment.)

11. Activate the front layers and print. Deactivate the front layers, activate the back layers, turn the sheet of paper over (but do not rotate) and print the reverse side.

12. Trim postcards to size.

13. (Opt.) Use a craft punch to add rounded corners.

NOTE

It's simple yet critical to drag out Guides and align layouts so that the front and reverse sides line up precisely once the cards are trimmed.

Mini Collage
Thank-you Notes

This project is really fun. Each card is a one-of-a-kind mini work of art with a spontaneous, effortless feeling. You can use gift wrap from the shower itself or any decorative papers. No need to print anything on the card this time—although you might want to sign the back of each piece, give it a title (e.g., Nicole's Baby Shower), or include the date of the shower.

These whimsical thank-you notes are enjoyable and simple to make.

You Will Need

- A favorite photo from the baby shower
- Glossy, pearl, or luster photo paper
- Decorative papers or wrapping paper (crumpled adds to the effect)
- Complementary ribbons or embellishments
- 140-pound watercolor paper
- Glue stick
- Bone folder
- Paper cutter
- Straightedge or ruler
- 4 3/8 x 5 3/4-inch envelopes

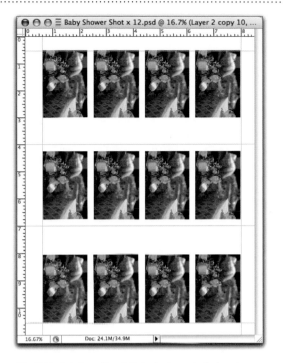

Use Guides to help you line up the twelve images in the layout.

1. Open an image file (300 ppi) and resize to 2 1/2 inches in width. Copy and paste or click and drag twelve copies into a new letter-sized file (300 ppi).

2 Drag out Guides as shown to help with alignment, moving each copy into precise position to minimize the number of cuts necessary to create twelve individual images with 1/8-inch borders.

3. Print, then trim each image to size. Close the original image file without saving it. Save the layered file to print additional copies or to use as a template for future projects.

4. Use a straightedge to help tear watercolor paper into 8 1/2 x 5 1/2-inch pieces, then fold each piece in half to create a 5 1/2 x 4 1/4-inch note card. Burnish the fold with the broad edge of a bone folder. (Whenever possible, preserve any natural deckled edges on the watercolor paper.)

5. Tear decorative papers into irregular shapes small enough to fit on the card. Glue one piece onto the card, allowing the edges to remain free, and then add another to create a mini collage. Glue an image on top and add a short length of ribbon or other embellishment.

CHAPTER 6

Hello, Baby: Newborns

There are few subjects as delightful to photograph as the newest and tiniest member of the family. You'll undoubtedly find yourself wanting to memorialize each and every facial expression for posterity—sleeping, yawning, smiling, even crying—and, oh, those delicate ears, that fine wisp of hair, those chubby hands and feet! Here are some ideas for capturing memorable images of this little bundle of love and turning those photos into charming birth announcements, brag books, and more.

Tips & Tricks for Photographing Babies

Although you may have preconceived notions of certain photos you plan to take, it's very likely that those specific photo ops may never present themselves. I love taking pictures of naked babies, but many newborns immediately begin to bawl when not swaddled. So toss your agenda aside and be attuned to authentic moments as they crop up naturally. Maybe it's a big brother or sister or even the family pet making an appearance at baby's side, or Mom nursing in a rocking chair next to a window. I'm even at the ready during diaper changing, hoping I'll catch that one-in-a-million shot—the look of surprise mixed with amusement and dismay when the little squirt springs a leak, hitting Mom or Dad in the face before the diaper's on! I think it happens at least once to every parent of a male child, but rarely when there's a camera around.

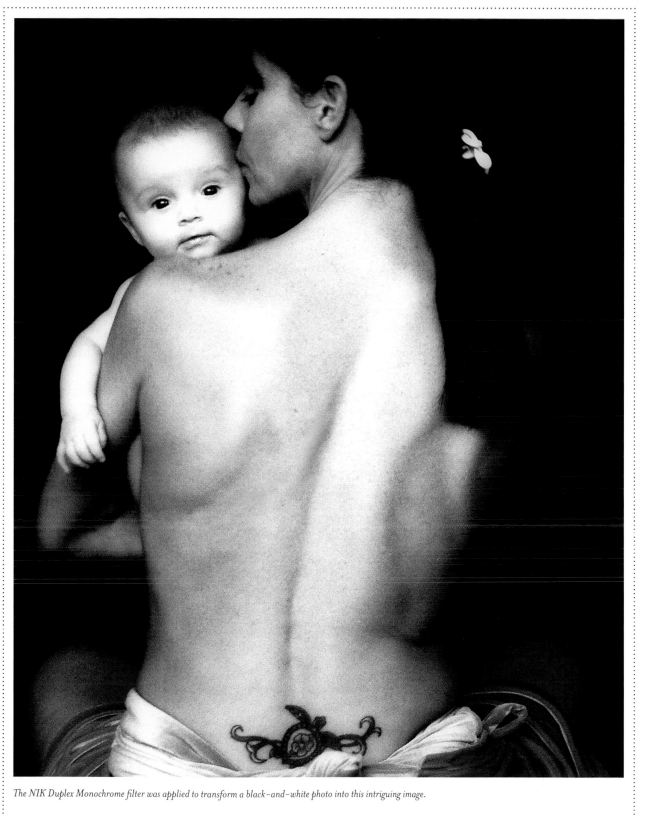

The NIK Duplex Monochrome filter was applied to transform a black-and-white photo into this intriguing image.

Shoot in Natural Light

I can't imagine shooting a newborn in anything but natural light. It means less cumbersome equipment and no flashes to disturb the baby. Newborns are especially sensitive to sound and light. Once the baby starts crying in earnest, the photo session may have to end prematurely. So in low light, use a tripod and load fast film or set your digital ISO as the conditions dictate. Of course, if the baby is asleep, you'll get sharper images shooting at an ISO of 200, even with a slow shutter speed.

Shooting in natural light means long exposures, and, unless they're asleep, babies are in constant motion. Of course, some movement, the kicking of tiny feet or the grasping of a chubby hand, can add a dynamic element to a shot.

Babies are most happy being held. Transforming this photo into black and white lessens the distraction of Mom's arms. Natural light coming in through a window enhances the softness and shadows. Can you imagine the difference if a flash had been used? Not nearly so pretty a picture!

Keep It Simple: Props and Backgrounds

Have solid-colored clean blankets or sheets nearby to spread on a bed, changing table, sofa, or floor, to hang as a backdrop, and/or to hide clutter if necessary. A black or off-white background best complements a baby's skin tone.

I'm not a big fan of props, but if you are, the best time to use them is when baby is sleeping. Faux flowers, butterflies, angel wings, and ribbons and bows are all things baby probably wouldn't tolerate when awake but that you might be able to get away with now. You might want to use classic props like stuffed animals, alphabet blocks, and rattles to add subtext. I try to avoid things like pacifiers ("binkies"), modern baby bottles, and anything sporting a brand name.

Here black flannel sheets were used as a background to minimize distraction and focus attention on the heart of the matter.

What to Wear
(Or Not to Wear)

It's best if anyone who will be in the photos wears solid colors, preferably black or off-white, as those provide the best backgrounds for close-ups when the baby is being held. Mom's nails should be neat, as the details of her hands may show in close-ups. As far as makeup, some light lipstick should suffice: It's not a glamour shot session, more like a soft environmental portrait. Dad can wear whatever he wants for cute shots with personality, showing the contrast between his strength and baby's vulnerability. Tattoos, muscles, powerful hands—great stuff! Or maybe Mom is the one with the tattoos and/or muscles, in which case

you may want to go for a much less traditional look. If she's in good shape after giving birth, she might want to have some tasteful nude studies made of her and the baby.

It's all about body language—baby's uncertainty, Dad's protective instinct, and the dog's natural curiosity. I love the contrast between the tattooed and newborn skin.

Twins present a unique compositional challenge—resolved in this case with a cropped panoramic format.
Clearly, the tasteful nudity and careful positioning makes this a standout shot that just about anyone would appreciate.

Get the Details

Sleeping babies are a joy to photograph. You can get as close as need be to capture the tender, miraculous details of "baby parts"—whirls and wisps of hair, exquisite ears, chubby arms and legs, porcelain hands and feet, luminous skin, dimples and wrinkles. Some babies sleep more soundly than others, allowing you to change their position to enhance the composition of the photo.

TIP

If you're shooting in color, you'll undoubtedly want to convert some of your images into black and white in postproduction. It's a great way to lessen the sometimes ruddy appearance of a newborn's skin, and it lends a timeless interpretation to the classic theme of mother and child.

I just can't resist the wrinkles . . . babies wear them so well! This shot owes much of its appeal to natural light and the black-and-white treatment.

A black-and-white treatment emphasizes the contrast between the father's strength and his child's vulnerability.

Capture the Love: Mother and Child

What could be a more fitting subject for fine art photography? The eternal feminine mystique, the ineffable bond between mother and child—be sure to capture the nurturing.

Capture the Rembrandt moment with the quiet light and the half-smile of the nurturing mother as she gazes down at her sleeping child.

Get skin, skin on skin, curves and crevices, the interplay between light and shadow. When being nurtured, hearing its mother's heartbeat, feeling her warmth, cradled in the security of her arms, the baby usually falls asleep. Get close, closer, and closer still.

Hospital Photos

Photographs taken in the hospital are not the best candidates for birth announcements. As a rule, the surroundings are ugly, the fluorescent lighting is ugly, the baby is, well, certainly not ugly, but at the very least probably red and puffy and not exactly photogenic at this point. On the other hand, friends and family are waiting eagerly for that first glimpse, making hospital shots perfect for e-mailing.

Classic Birth Announcement

Sweet and endearing but not necessarily cute—that was my intention in designing this birth announcement. The challenge lay in combining a number of separate elements in such a way as to produce a seemingly simple, unified design. For instance, it was necessary to lower the opacity of the background text layer to such an extent that it didn't "fight" with the important data surrounding the image.

An alternative to cute, this elegant birth announcement features subtle "poetry" that adds an emotional component. Newborns are often ruddy; a black-and-white treatment remedies that. (Gill Sans)

You Will Need

- A photo
- Your choice of photo printing paper: glossy, matte, or pearl/luster
- Paper cutter or craft knife
- Ruler
- Self-healing cutting mat
- 5 ¼ x 5 ¼-inch envelopes

1. Create a new file (File>New) with a custom size of 5 x 5 inches (300 ppi).

2. Choose the Type tool and type a poem or some meaningful text. Select the text, and select a script font (the sample uses P22 Cezanne, 72 point, with 72-point leading). Go to Edit>Transform>Rotate and, in the Options bar, specify a minus 25 (or -25) rotation. Press Return/Enter to apply the transformation. Use the Move tool to nudge the text into place. In the Layers palette, reduce the layer opacity to around 20 percent.

3. Open an image file. (If the image is color, convert it to black and white. See page 50.) If necessary, crop and/or resize the image to 2 1/2 x 2 1/2 inches.

4. Drag the image into the new file (or copy and paste), and close the original image file without saving it. In the new file, go to Edit>Stroke and add a 2-pixel border to the outside of the image.

5. Create the text "border": Click on the Type tool, select an easy-to-read font and type the text for the top border, and then move it into position. Double-click on the T thumbnail in the Layers palette to select (highlight) the type and, in the Text Character palette, adjust the tracking (the space between the characters) as necessary. Add a new layer and type the text for the right side of the border. Go to Edit>Transform>Rotate 90° CW, move it into position, and adjust the tracking. Add another new layer and type the text for the left side of the border; go to Edit>Transform>Rotate 90° CCW (counter-

clockwise), move it into position, and adjust the tracking. Follow the same procedure for the bottom border, but move it into position without rotating it.

6. To add a subtle background color, in the Layers palette, create a new layer above the Background layer. In the Toolbox, set the Foreground color to red or blue, and use the Paint Bucket tool to fill the layer with color, and then lower the layer opacity to 8 to 20 percent.

7. Flatten the layout file *but do not save it.*

8. (Opt.) If you've opted for a white background, you may want to print a cutting guide: Go to Select>All, or press Command/Control + A. Go to Edit>Stroke and choose a 1-pixel black inside stroke.

9. Copy and paste (or click and drag) two copies into a letter-size sheet of paper and move them into position, making sure no part of the layout falls within the area outside the printable margins. (To keep them in vertical alignment, thus eliminating extra cutting strokes, hold down the Shift key when moving them.)

10. Go back to the original file, revert to the unflattened version, and save.

11. Print and trim to size.

Film Strip
Birth Announcement

In this clever announcement, the use of transparency film mimics the look of a 35mm negative film strip, even though the images aren't negatives at all but digital photos. You can make your own blank film strip by scanning a piece of exposed film, or you can go to my website and download mine at www.bsmithphotograpy.com/goodies. Experiment with formats, fonts, and fasteners for different effects.

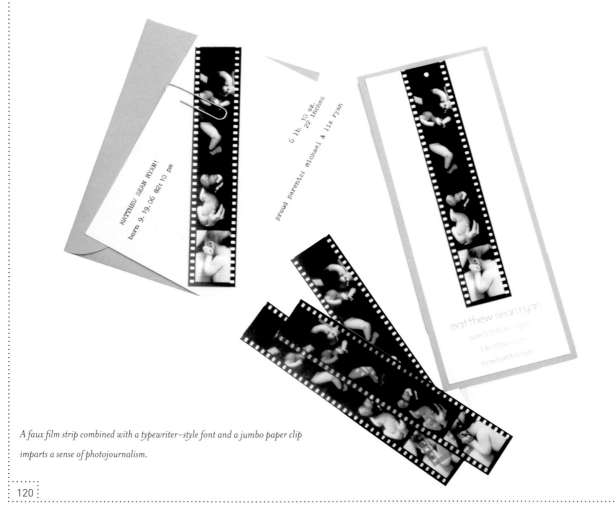

A faux film strip combined with a typewriter-style font and a jumbo paper clip imparts a sense of photojournalism.

You Will Need

- 3M Multipurpose Transparency Film
- Heavyweight matte printing paper
- Fastener (brad, eyelet, paper clip, etc.)
- Four photos of the newborn
- Paper cutter or craft knife
- Metal ruler
- Cutting mat
- Envelopes

1. Scan a length of 35mm film at 300 ppi. Go to Edit>Adjustments>Levels and adjust the image using the sliders so that it's dark black and bright white. Save the file and keep it open.

2. Open a 300 ppi image, resize it to 1 x 1½ inches, and copy and paste or drag it into the open window containing the film strip. Do the same with three more images. (Note: Use black and white photos. To convert color images to black and white, see page 50.)

3. Drag the images into place on the film strip, leaving a 1/8-inch space between them. If the images don't fit precisely within the sprocket "holes," with the appropriate layer highlighted, go to Edit>Transform>Scale and drag the handles to resize as needed.

4. Go to Image>Flatten Layers and click OK. Go to Image>Rotate Canvas>Flip Canvas Horizontal.

NOTE

Owing to the nature of the transparency sheet, you will be printing on the textured, or "wrong," side; by flipping the canvas, the image will appear in its correct configuration when you look at the smooth "right" side.)

5. To conserve time and materials, print several strips on one sheet of film: Open a new letter-size file (with a resolution of 300 ppi), and drag the film strip in, positioning it toward the left side of the sheet, then press Option/Alt + Shift and click and drag additional copies across the sheet as shown. Print the images, then trim each film strip to size.

The "film strip" layout.

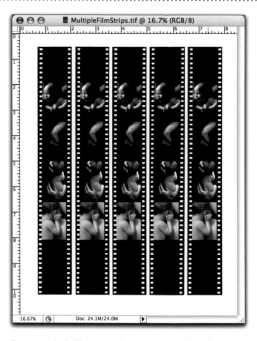

Printing multiple film strips will conserve materials and make it easy to create lots of announcements.

6. Open a new 5 x 7-inch file. Click on the Type (T) tool and lay out the text.

TIP

For ease in repositioning and formatting text elements (baby's name, weight, etc.), type each element on a separate layer.

---

7. Once you're satisfied with the layout, save the layered file. Then flatten the image. Go to Select>All. Now go to Edit>Stroke, choose a 2-pixel black stroke and choose Inside. (This will give you an outline to use as a cutting guide.) Go to Edit>Copy.

8. Open a new letter-size file. Drag out Guides 1/2 inch from the top and 1/2 inch from the bottom of the page. Go to Edit>Paste, and, holding down the Shift key, drag the layout into the upper half of the page so that the upper edge is flush with the upper Guide. Go to Edit>Paste once more, hold down the Shift key, and drag the second layout into the lower half of the page so that the lower edge is flush with the lower Guide.

9. Print, and cut out cards using the borders as a cutting guide. Attach the film strip.

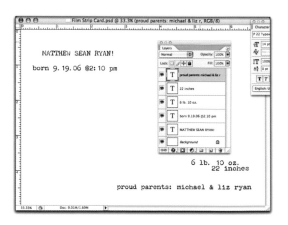

Laying out the announcement using different layers for each line of text.

A Few More Ideas

- If most of your photos are vertical, lay out the card in a vertical format.
- For a striking presentation, create a 3 7/8 x 9 3/4-inch layout, attach the film strip with an eyelet, and enclose the announcement in an open-end catalog envelope with a string closure.
- Increase the size and/or color of the stroke to create and include a decorative border.

Cigar Tin Birth Announcement

Cigars are traditionally passed out upon the birth of a baby. This clever announcement gives a nod to that custom while taking it one step further by decorating a miniature cigar tin with a photo of the little one on the cover and a few more shots inside. Parents can also use the tin to hold keepsake items such as a lock of hair or a baby bracelet.

Small or miniature cigars come in shallow decorative containers, usually eight to a pack. The craftsmanship is really quite nice—even the paper insert is charming. If you don't happen to know a cigar smoker, see if your friendly local smoke shop will allow you to leave a handful of business cards on the counter requesting that patrons call you to collect their empties.

You Will Need

- Photos
- Cigar tin
- Acrylic craft paint
- Sponge brush
- Flat-bottomed dish or jar lid
- Craft glue
- Decorative paper in various patterns, colors, etc.
- Metal label holder and decorative brad
- Wire
- Asian coins (with square holes in the middle—available at many craft and bead stores)
- Embellishments (flowers, mini origami pieces, etc.)
- Heavyweight paper
- Bone folder
- Ruler
- Self-healing cutting mat
- Corner rounder
- Double-stick photo mount squares

Decorate the cover and add a photo. Embellish with coins, charms, faux gems,

ribbon, alphabet letters, a tag—whatever strikes your fancy.

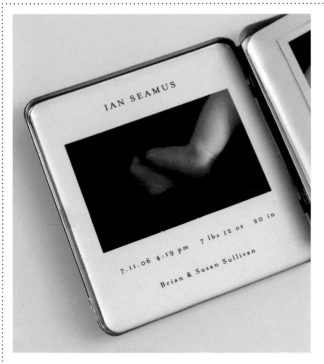

The layout for the announcement itself was designed in Photoshop.

6. Run the dangling ends of the wire through the hole in an Asian coin to attach it. Link a second coin to the first one.

7. Glue additional elements (e.g., an origami crane and paper flowers) to the collage.

8. In Photoshop, create a layout for an announcement the same size as the interior dimensions of the lid. Include the baby's name, birth date, weight and size, etc. Print and trim. Use the corner rounder to trim the corners. Adhere the announcement to the inside of the lid.

9. To create the insert, cut a long strip of water-color paper to the height of the tin and 16 inches long.

10. Using a bone folder and ruler, accordion-fold the paper at 4-inch intervals.

11. Using the corner rounder, trim each corner of the folded insert.

12. Using double-stick tape, add photos to each page.

13. Glue the back of the last panel to the inside back cover of the tin, to secure the insert.

1. Remove paper labels such as price tags and bar codes, leaving the broken paper seal in place as a collage element.

2. Paint the tin and allow it to dry thoroughly.

3. Using craft glue, adhere a piece of decorative paper to the top. Tear smaller pieces of paper and collage on top.

4. Glue a small photo into a metal label holder. Insert a decorative brad into one of the holes of the metal label holder, run a 12-inch length of wire (bent in the middle) through the other hole, then twist the wire near the hole to secure it.

5. Use craft glue to affix the frame to the tin.

TIP

Instead of manually adhering the photos to the insert, you could lay out the insert in Photoshop.

Handcrafted Brag Book

This elegant little photo album is easily tucked into a purse or briefcase—perfect for new moms, dads, and grandparents. Use photo corners or double-sided tape to insert up to twenty-four 4 x 6-inch photos inside. Optionally, lay out the pages in Photoshop and print onto photo-quality paper.

You Will Need

- 140-pound watercolor paper for cover
- Sturdy paper for pages (e.g., Canson Mi-Teintes)
- Tie (ribbon, thread, or cord)
- Fastener (button or bead)
- Hole punch or awl (size to accommodate tie material)
- Scissors
- Bone folder
- Paper cutter or craft knife
- Ruler
- Self-healing cutting mat

1. To make the cover, cut or tear the watercolor paper to $15\frac{1}{2}$ x $4\frac{5}{8}$ inches. Score as indicated in the template (see page 128) and fold panel A toward the center. Fold panel C toward the center, overlapping panel A.

2. To make the pages, cut six sheets of paper to 13 x $4\frac{1}{2}$ inches. Fold each sheet in half horizontally and nest together to create a twenty-four-page "signature." Trim the edges so that they're perfectly flush.

TIP

When working with large sheets of paper, it's helpful to use an oversized cutting mat (such as those commonly used for laying out clothing patterns) in conjunction with an extra long metal ruler or straightedge.

The deckled edge of a sheet of pink watercolor paper and a sparkly bead enhance the album on top. Natural white watercolor paper was torn to make the cover for the center album. For the bottom album, apple green momi *paper was adhered to and wrapped around a cardboard substrate, and a colorful complementary liner provides a neat finish.*

Brag book template.

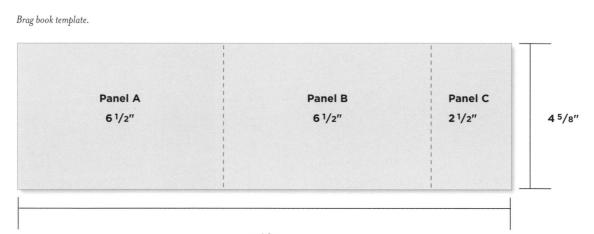

Panel A	Panel B	Panel C
6 1/2"	6 1/2"	2 1/2"

4 5/8"

15 1/2"

3. Nest the signature into the fold created between cover panels A and B, centering the pages between the top and bottom.

4. Punch holes through the entire assembly 1 inch in from the top and 1 inch in from the bottom.

5. Cut the tie to 18 inches, then thread it through one hole from the outside to the inside and then out through the other hole. Tie a tight knot at the center of the outside spine.

6. Affix the button to the front center of folded panel C by punching two holes and then running a length of ribbon, fiber, or thread through the bead and threading it through the holes, then knotting it securely on the inside. (If desired, hide the knot with a "patch" made of watercolor paper.)

7. Pull the ends of tie snugly over the bead and tie into a knot, then trim.

A Few More Ideas

This project lends itself to endless creative interpretation by simply substituting papers and embellishments.

- As in the bottom album in the photograph on page 127, substitute cardboard or plain card stock for the watercolor paper and cover with handmade or decorative paper. Adhere a decorative liner to the inside of the cover to finish.
- Mount a photo on the cover as a layered unit, as in the middle album in the photograph.
- Cut out a window that frames a key area of the photograph appearing on the first page (e.g., baby's eyes or fingers).
- Add a nameplate or spell out the baby's name with mini alphabet blocks.

Personalized Compact Discs & DVDs

Chances are you'll have more than just one photo of the little one you'd love to share with family and friends. An easy way to do this is to put the best images on a CD or DVD. Recipients can then print their favorite photos. Be sure to adhere a custom label to the disc itself to up the "WOW!" factor.

You Will Need

- Digital images
- CD or DVD
- Self-adhesive CD/DVD labels

A custom CD/DVD label adds a personal touch to electronic media. You might also want to design your own jewel case cover and insert.

Making Adjustments

These instructions are for standard CD/DVD labels available at computer and office supply stores and printed on an Epson inkjet printer. Because of variations between printers, slight adjustments to the layout may be necessary. After you have created a label, print a test on a sheet of plain paper. Place a sheet of blank labels in front of it and hold it up to the light. If the printed layout does not line up precisely with the label, unlock the layers in the Layers palette and use the arrow keys on your keyboard to nudge things into proper position. Relock the layers and save the tweaked version.

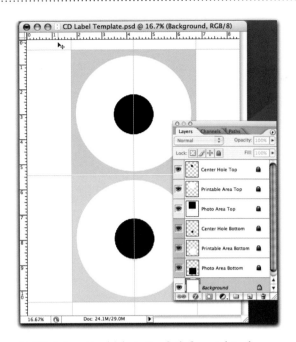

You'll be laying out two labels at a time. In the Layers palette, the layers highlighted in yellow relate to the top template, and the layers highlighted in green relate to the bottom template.

1. Go to www.bsmithphotography.com/goodies and download the file named "CD-DVD Label Template." Open the file in Photoshop. You'll use the shapes, or zones, as an aid in aligning the graphic elements for your own label. Go to View>Show>Guides to turn Guides on and off.

2. Open the file containing the image you would like to use on your CD/DVD label. If necessary crop and/or resize the image so the height is 5 inches. The resolution should be 300 ppi.

3. Click and drag the image into the CD/DVD Label Template. In the Layers palette, click on this new layer. If it's not already at the top of the palette, drag it to the top, and lower the opacity so that you can see the preexisting layers beneath it in the open window. Close the original image file *without saving it*.

4. Use the arrow keys to move the image into place within the template. For a "bleed"—in other words, if you want the entire label to be filled with image—make sure that there are no important details outside the circular white "safe" zone and that there is no white space remaining within that zone. Keep in mind that there will be a hole where the black area is.

   If you prefer not to have a bleed, just resize the image: With the Move tool (V) activated, click on the image layer, go to Edit>Transform>Scale and type in percentages in the Options bar, or drag the handles to resize. Allow the white background to show, or add a new layer below it and use

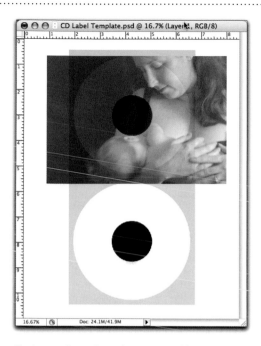

Use the arrow keys to finesse the positioning of the image within the template so that nothing important gets cut off.

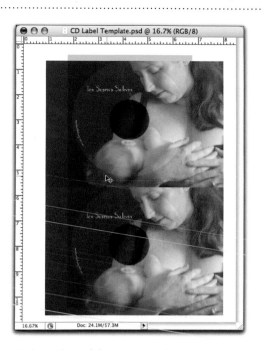

As always, it's a good idea to print more than one piece at a time to save time and money.

the Paint Bucket tool (G) to fill it with color. (The Paint Bucket may be nesting beneath the Gradient tool in the Toolbox.)

5. Click on the Type tool (T) and add text. If you have more than one text block (e.g. title, date, birth information), it's a good idea to type each on a separate layer to be formatted and moved around as needed. To make the text conform to the shape of the disc (as I did with my website address), go to Edit>Transform>Rotate to change the position or angle of the type, then use Text Warp (Arc) to create the curve (see "Creating Warped Text" on page 37).

6. Once you're satisfied with the layout, and if you plan to print two labels, in the Layers palette, select the visible layers and then drag them down to the Create a New

Layer icon to the right of the trash can at the bottom of the Layers palette. Then, in the open window, use the Move tool to drag the new layout into place in the bottom template.

7. In the Layers palette, reset the opacity for the image layers to 100 percent, and toggle the eye icons to hide the visibility of the preexisting layers if they happen to show in the window.

8. Print the labels using a quality setting for plain paper and save the file under a new name.

TIP

To conserve ink, before printing, use the Eraser tool to eliminate portions of the image that fall outside the label area.

CHAPTER 7

Small Wonders: Toddlers and Beyond

Have you ever wondered whether your earliest memories are actual memories or pseudo memories evoked by a photograph in an old family album? Childhood is fleeting, and even as we try to hold on to our recollections, they are gradually replaced by more recent events and developments. The more photos you take of the children in your life, the better chance you have of committing those moments to memory—yours *and* theirs. Turning those photos into cards, books, calendars, and more will ensure no precious memory is lost.

Taking Better Family Photos

When my grandmother was a child growing up in Chicago, a traveling photographer would come to town from time to time and spend the day photographing her and her sisters. I'm charmed by the imaginative photos he took of them perched among the branches of a tree, posing in the park, sitting in a boat at the lake, and "vogue-ing" on the steps of the brownstone they lived in.

Today's equivalent to those types of images would be what have come to be known in the photography industry as "day in the life" photos. There's been an explosion in the popularity of day-in-the-life photo sessions akin to the spread of photojournalistic wedding photography. The idea is to catch the family, particularly the children, in their natural element doing what they might do on an ordinary day when there's no photographer around. Even if you're not a pro, you can use some of the same ideas to capture memorable photos of your own family.

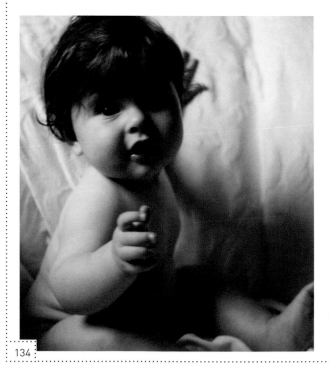

The skin of a young child is one of the wonders of the world, and the most effective way of capturing it is also the simplest—through the use of natural light.

A Day in the Life

It's really quite amazing to think of the myriad classic photos ops you might encounter on any given day in the life of a family at home. Look for the extraordinary in the seemingly ordinary:

- Getting ready for school: brushing hair, tying shoes, buttoning coats
- Doing homework or reading a book
- Playing with a pet or with friends
- Putting on skates or athletic shoes
- Playing a game or sport, running through sprinklers, or riding a skateboard
- Flying a kite, blowing bubbles, playing marbles, blowing at a dandelion, or climbing a tree
- Music or dance lessons; playing an instrument or wearing a tutu
- Making an art project

- Playing in the backyard: on a climbing structure, slide, or swing
- In the garden, sitting under a tree, picking a flower, playing in the mud
- Asleep in the car or under an umbrella, under a hat, or behind sunglasses
- Looking out the window
- Bath time; hair being shampooed, brushed, or braided; getting ready for bed
- Having a bandage applied to a boo-boo

Capturing the Mood

There's a story behind every picture. Capture the innocence. Look for those real-life moments and scenarios that will be looked back upon someday and evoke a sense of nostalgia for time gone by. Include pensive as well as playful, sad as well as glad. A photo of a child crying may be as treasured as of one laughing with joy in years to come.

A photo of a little girl in the simple act of picking a flower evokes the innocence of childhood.

Family Interactions

When there's more than one child in the family, be sure to include the interaction be-tween them—an arm draped across shoulders, holding hands, hugging, heads close together in a whisper, riding piggyback. Don't forget to get shots of the kids on Dad's shoulders, in Mom's lap, and holding simple props like a teddy bear, doll, or ball.

A spontaneous kiss that speaks volumes about the nature of brotherly love.

On the merry-go-round with great-grandmother. A black-and white treatment turns this shot into an instant classic.

Clothes

It's best if family members wear clothing that is somewhat coordinated. They don't have to be matchy-matchy, but maybe everyone could go barefoot; wear jeans and T-shirts; dress in black, white, or khaki; or wear clothing in a similar solid color or two. Try to avoid clothing with prominent slogans or logos: Our eyes go right to that type of thing the moment we first glance at a photograph.

Three brothers all wearing shirts of a different stripe produced a dynamic effect.

Location and Backgrounds

Scout out areas with lots of natural light and a minimum of background distraction. Of course some things can be moved aside, but piles of papers and tangled electronic cords should be avoided. On the other hand, children's rooms, even when cluttered, can provide apt settings. Pianos are a slam-dunk—classic theme, clas-sic lines. The same goes for outdoor things like bikes and trikes, scooters and wagons. Some children's furniture—small tables and chairs, easels, and beds—make great props, but modern high chairs and playpens leave something to be desired in terms of aesthetics.

Use sofas for groupings and for effective horizontal shots. Stairs can also be put to good use for group shots, and other architectural elements, such as windows and doors, may make perfect frames. Bookshelves make nice backgrounds; TVs not so much, but a shot of a kid watching TV or working at the computer will tell the story of a particular pastime in this child's life.

Details, Details, Details

As always, but especially when shooting children, get close, and then get closer. Capture the glow of youthful skin, the deep, clear eyes, the sun-kissed curls. Or the scrapes and scratches, the dirty faces, hands, or feet. Another benefit of getting closer? Less background to deal with. At the same time, use details, such as a favorite toy, comic book or, temporary tattoo to tell the story.

Toning a black-and-white image using the Hue/Saturation method (see page 51) heightens the impact of this shot inspired by the old bathtub and art deco tile work. Certain themes are classic, and this is certainly one of them.

TIP

If you're planning on memorializing a day, life, or year in a handmade book (see next page), be sure to capture some scene setters and details—refrigerator art, easels, dolls and stuffed animals, patchwork quilts, piano music, shelves filled with books or games, the garden. These images can be used to add interest to the book or as backgrounds on which to place other photos.

Practicing on the same old piano Dad learned to play on. The dominance of the instrument provides a strong counterpoint to the intent gaze of the young musician in this "environmental portrait."

Dirty feet and an abandoned teddy—it's been a long day. A sleeping child makes for a particularly poignant image.

Mixed-media Books

You can buy hard- and soft-cover books of your photos online through sites like Shutterfly.com, MyPublisher.com, and KodakGallery.com or design them on your Mac using iPhoto, but a handcrafted book is almost as quick and easy with the added benefit that you get to control the size, shape, and number of pages. More important, handcrafted books offer a dimension of warmth and thoughtful attention to detail that's missing from commercially printed books. Keep it simple: clean layouts with just a few photos on a page, and snippets of text rather than entire paragraphs.

You Will Need

- Lots of photo files
- Plain paper for mockup
- Double-sided matte photo paper (letter size)
- Paper cutter, scissors, or craft knife
- Heavy vellum or card stock for covers
- Ruler
- Bone folder
- Inexpensive card stock for punch template
- Hole punch
- Small binder clips
- Your choice of vellum, acetate, and/or decorative papers for overlays (optional)
- Embroidery needle
- Cord, ribbon, or waxed linen bookbinding thread
- Beads or other embellishments (optional)

Mix It Up

Not just for photos, a mixed-media book is the perfect place to display other family memorabilia. Here are a few ideas. Keep in mind that if you don't want to use the originals, you can always copy or scan and print them.

- Child's artwork
- Homework pages
- Sonograms
- Favorite family expressions or quotes
- Homemade greeting cards
- Report cards and/or progress reports
- Calendar pages
- Grocery and to-do lists

Combine fun papers, fonts, and embellishments with family photos and memorabilia

for a truly unique mixed-media artbook.

1. Create a master page layout that is 6 inches wide by 5 inches tall (300 ppi, RGB). Drag out Guides 1 inch in from each side margin.

   You'll use this file to create each page of the book, renaming it appropriately each time (e.g., Page 1, Page 2, Beach Day, Vacation).

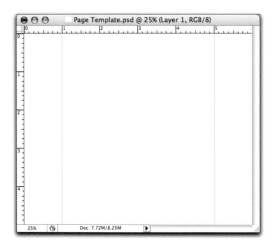

Basic page layout with Guides.

2. Design your pages using the tips and techniques found throughout this book, making sure that each photo you bring into a layout is also 300 ppi. For each page of the book that you want to open/appear to the *right* of the spine, none of your layout should fall within the 1-inch spine area delineated by the left-hand Guide. For these pages, your design should extend all the way to the right edge.

   For each page of the book that will open/appear to the *left* of the spine, make sure nothing falls within the 1-inch area on the right-hand side. Save each page with its own name.

> **NOTE**
> These instructions are for a 6 x 5-inch book. For a larger book, simply modify the dimensions as appropriate throughout, taking your paper size and printer limitations into consideration.

You can either print single photos (with or without text) or create digital scrapbook pages like these. Have fun with journaling, adding colored or textured backgrounds, layering, changing opacity, and using any of the graphic techniques presented in this book. (Font: Lemonade)

Mock It Up

To help figure out the order of your pages, it is *very* helpful to make a miniature mockup to use as a reference for the final book layout. After you've designed and saved all the pages in one folder, print contact sheets on plain paper using the Automate function in Photoshop (File>Automate>Contact Sheet II) (say twelve to sixteen layouts per letter-size sheet).

Trim each image to size, then play with the arrangement. Decide if you want to arrange the images chronologically. Think about which pages will face each other. You might want to place certain pages next to each other to create a two-page spread. Although the final book will be printed on both sides of the paper, it's not necessary to print on both sides at this point, but you may want to adhere the pages back-to-back to make sure there are no "blanks."

Making a rough mockup to determine page order is especially helpful when printing double-sided pages.

3. To print in Photoshop: Go to File>Page Setup and choose a letter-size page and the standard portrait orientation.

    Go to File>Print with Preview, specify a 0.25-inch margin at the top of the sheet, and leave the left margin as it is (it should say 1.125 inches). This ensures that both sides of the page will be perfectly aligned when printed. It will also leave you with enough room to print another page on the remainder of the paper.

    Now click on Print and proceed as you would normally (e.g., choose the proper paper and photo print quality in the print settings menu).

4. Trim each page to size, *remembering to leave the 1-inch white margin at the spine edge.*

5. Use heavy vellum or card stock for the front and back covers, and, if you wish, make them just a tiny bit larger than the pages. Use a ruler and bone folder to score a fold line on the front cover 1 inch from the left edge. Don't fold the cover per se, but bend it just slightly along the scored line to give the impression of a spine.

6. (Opt.) Randomly intersperse pages with a few 6 x 5-inch vellum or acetate overlays to add color and texture.

7. Make a punch template by cutting a piece of heavy card stock to the same size as the covers of the book, and then punch two holes 1 inch in from the spine edge and 1¼ inches from the top and bottom of the book. Place the template over each page in turn, including the covers, and punch through the holes.

A punch template will help you line up all the pages perfectly.

8. Assemble the book and clamp the covers and pages together to hold in place while stitching the binding. Thread the binding material on the needle and insert the needle into the top hole in the front cover, leaving a tail long enough to tie into a bow.

9. Wrap the thread over the top edge of the book and reenter the same hole, pulling the thread taut.

Wrapping the thread around the top edge of the book and pulling it through the same hole second time (see step 9).

10. Wrap the thread around the spine edge and enter the same hole once again, exiting through the back cover.

Wrapping the thread around the spine as in step 10.

11. Drawing the thread firmly across the back cover, pull it up through the second hole.

12. Wrap the thread around the spine edge and through the hole from the back.

13. Wrap the thread around the bottom edge of the book and once again through the hole from the back.

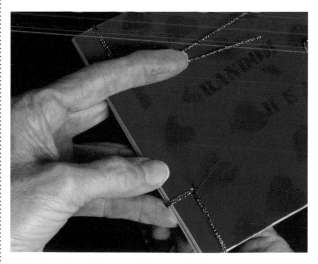

Pull the thread through the bottom hole to finish binding the bottom corner (see step 13).

14. Tie the ends of the thread firmly in a bow or knot and, optionally, hang beads or other embellishments.

A Few More Ideas

Have fun by combining the bookmaking basics above with an off-the-wall and over-the-top creative technique.

- Use the hole punch to make additional holes, then connect the pages with binder rings or large jump rings instead of the edge-stitched binding. Tie ribbon or fiber onto the rings to add pizzazz.
- For a funky grunge style, make an accordion book by using gaffer's tape, masking tape, colored tape, or metallic tape to join the pages to each other back and front.
- Decorate the cover with a collage and/or three-dimensional embellishments.

TIP

While you're laying out pages, why not borrow a few elements—say, three images and a line of text—to create a note card or letterhead, then print a dozen copies. There are still lots of people keeping in touch with family and friends via snail mail, and while e-mail may be easier and faster, receiving "real" mail makes people feel special.

Custom Birthday Invitations

Why buy a box of ordinary invitations when you can easily whip up extraordinary ones that show off a photo (or two or three) of the birthday boy or girl? This layout is designed to fit into a square envelope, but you can just as easily start with a horizontal or vertical format slightly smaller than the size of any standard envelope. Feel free to mix up the design, moving elements around to suit yourself.

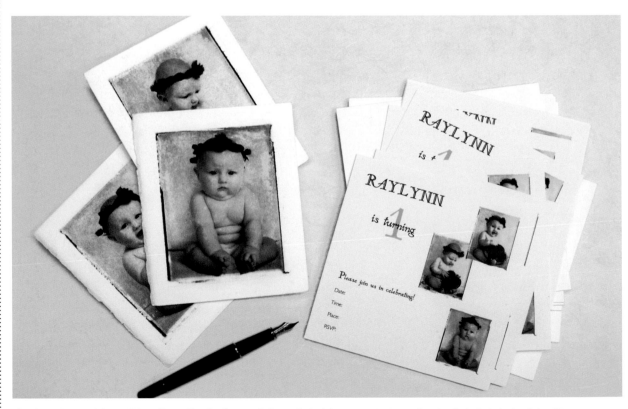

Transforming 35mm slides into Polaroid Image Transfers (see page 63) gives this birthday party invitation a truly unique look. An invitation designed in Photoshop will still convey the warmth of the personal touch when the party specifics are filled in by hand. (Fonts: Interlude and Gill Sans Light)

You Will Need
- **One to three photos of the guest of honor**
- **Heavyweight matte printing paper**
- **Paper cutter**
- **6 x 6-inch envelopes**

1. Choose File>New and create a custom-size file of 5.75 x 5.75 inches with a resolution of 300 ppi. Select a color mode, usually RGB.

2. Drag out Guides of 1/4 inch from all edges.

3. Open the image files. If a file contains layers, flatten it. If an image needs to be resized, go to Image>Size and resize it to *approximately* the size you need—you'll have further opportunities to resize it. Make sure the images are the same resolution as the new file (300 ppi).

4. Drag the images into the new file. Go to Edit>Transform>Scale and resize each again if necessary. Use the Move tool (V) to slide the images into position within the area bound by the Guides. Note that in the Layers palette, each image is on its own layer; you can edit them (adjust the color, contrast, etc.), move them, or resize them at any time.

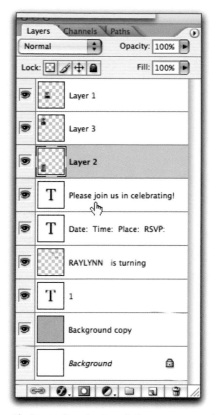

The Layers palette, showing each element as a separate layer.

5. Select the Type tool (I) and type the text. To format the text, in the Layers palette, double-click on the T thumbnail in the layer containing the text, then choose a font family, style, size, and color. Add a new layer for each text element so that you can edit it, move it, or resize it at any time, until or unless the file is flattened and closed, by first clicking on that layer.

6. If desired, use a small Brush (B) at 50-percent opacity or less to add subtle lines (see page 78).

7. Print and trim the invitation to size and save the layered file to use as a template for future projects.

Holiday Photo Cards

Family photo cards are a perennial favorite, but why be constrained by the limited selection of borders and formats available at quick print shops or online when it's soooo easy to print cards exactly as *you* want them?

The cover of this tent-style greeting card features a family portrait presented in a unique way—as text! Here the photo was enhanced with a Nik Multimedia filter (Duplex Color), but the impact can be just as dynamic with a full-color, black-and-white, or toned photo. Readability is key: Choose a "fat" font for the main word. These instructions are for a standard 7 x 5-inch (folded size) card.

This layout can be adapted to suit just about any holiday or occasion. For example, it could just as easily say "Season's Greetings" or "Happy Hanukkah." (Fonts: Bauhaus Heavy and Bauhaus Light)

You Will Need

- **A photo**
- **Double-sided matte photo paper***
- **Ruler**
- **Bone folder**
- **Envelopes (5 x 7 inches)**
  *Note: Use letter-size paper and trim after printing.

1. Choose File>New, under Preset choose Custom, and create a 7 x 10-inch file. The mode should be RGB Color and the resolution 300 ppi. From the top Ruler, drag out a Guide at 5 inches, and from the side Ruler, drag out Guides at ½ inch and 6 ½ inches to assist in the layout. (Guides will not appear on printed piece.) Save the new file, but don't close it.

2. Open the file containing the photograph you would like to incorporate in the layout. If the file contains layers, flatten the image. Make sure the resolution is 300 ppi. The width of the photo should be no more than 7 inches, although you will have the opportunity to resize it as necessary later on. With the Move tool (V) activated, click on the image and, holding down the Shift key, drag it into your previously opened file. Holding down the Shift key centers the photo within the new window. Even though part of the photograph may extend into the ½-inch side margin, as you'll see, it doesn't matter because it won't show; just make sure nothing important lies in that area.

   Close the *original* image file *without saving it.*

3. Now drag the image into position under the horizontal Guide as shown.

Positioning the image using Guides.

4. Click on the Type tool (T), then click anywhere in the upper half of the layout. Choose a font style and size (e.g., Bauhaus Heavy—150 pixels), then type the text. Click on the Move tool and drag the text into position over the photograph in the lower half of the layout. Use the arrow keys to position the text precisely where you want it, making sure nothing falls within the ½-inch side margins. As you'll soon see, you'll have unlimited opportunities to tweak the placement of both the text and the photo.

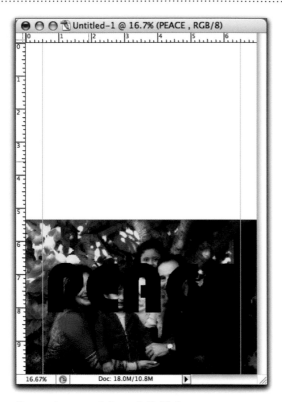

Dragging the text into the bottom half of the layout.

go to Edit>Transform>Scale, and use the handles to and resize the photo as necessary. Use the arrow keys as well to tweak the placement. When you're satisfied, press Return/Enter.

- To adjust the size and spacing of the text, double-click on the T icon next to the text layer in the Layers palette. In the Character palette (if it isn't visible, go to the Window menu and check Character), adjust the font size and tracking (the space between the letters). Click on the Move tool to disengage the Type tool.

5. In the Layers palette, click on the layer containing the text and drag it under the photo layer.

6. Here comes the fun part! Hold down the Option/Alt key and, in the Layers palette, click on the line between the text layer and the photo layer. Ta-da and voilà—the photo now fills the letters! (It may take a few clicks to hit it just right.)

7. Now use a combination of the processes described below to finesse the layout to perfection:

- To adjust the placement of the photo within the text outline, with the photo layer highlighted in the Layers palette,

8. Click on the Type tool to add another layer, and type the secondary text. Again, double-click on the T icon in the Layers palette and use the options in the Character palette to finesse the new text so that it lines up with the existing text.

9. Print the card using the best photo printer settings.

10. Trim $^3/_4''$ off each side and $^1/_2''$ off the top and bottom of the sheet, then fold the card in half. Cover the fold with a piece of scrap paper and burnish with the broad edge of a bone folder to flatten smoothly. (For heavier card stock, use the pointed end of the bone folder to score a fold line before folding.)

> *TIP*
>
> As always, print rough drafts on plain paper. Trim and fold as you would the final piece to make sure the layout is perfect. If not, tweak as needed.

Customizing Your Holiday Cards

Go to your local stationery store and check out the holiday cards. Using the techniques you've learned in this book, my guess is by now you could probably emulate just about any one of them! Of course, anything you create should reflect your own personal flair.

- For a festive border, scan some wrapping paper and, in Photoshop, use it as the bottom layer, placing a smaller photo on top, or just copy and paste a portion of it into your layout.

  Use complementary decorative fonts and colorful ink appropriate to the holiday being celebrated.
- Transform photos, including your personal "stock" images, into Polaroid image transfers (see page 63).
- In Photoshop, mix channels for a whimsical fine art effect (see page 56).
- Attach a simple embellishment such as ribbon, fiber, a twig, or a charm for a handcrafted touch.
- Add subtle gilding to watercolor or fine art digital paper by running the tip of a Marvy Liquid Gold or Liquid Silver opaque paint marker along the outside edge. This technique is particularly effective with deckled edges!

Adding a simple embellishment like a bow adds even more warmth to a personalized holiday greeting.

Gift Tags

Making tags is an art form in itself—seriously! Artist-designed tags are big business. Now *you* can make them. They're perfect for dressing up your holiday gifts, and so simple and fun to create you won't want to stop. Make them any size or shape you want. If you like, attach a tiny ornament, a charm, or a few beads. Gift tags are perfect for collage: Use glue to add three-dimensional embellishments like holly berries, beads, holiday trim, shells, skeleton leaves, or dried flowers.

Gift tags are so much fun to make, and recipients will want to hang on to these.

You Will Need

- One or more photos
- Heavyweight matte photo paper
- Paper cutter or craft knife
- Ruler
- Self-healing cutting mat
- $1/8$-inch hole punch
- Avery self-adhesive hole reinforcements; or eyelet setter, eyelets, and rubber mallet (optional)
- Complementary ribbon, raffia, cord, or string

1. Create a custom 2 x 3 1/2-inch Photoshop file (300 ppi).

2. Lay out a simple graphic design incorporating an image and text. The layout can be vertical or horizontal; for a horizontal layout, rotate the canvas 90° clockwise (Image>Rotate Canvas>90° CW).

3. Go to Layer>Flatten Image to flatten the file.

4. Open a new letter-size file and drag out Guides to divide it into twelve equal 2 x 3 1/2-inch segments as shown. Copy and paste or click and drag the tag file into the new file ten times, aligning the edges with the Guides.

   Optionally, follow steps 1 through 3 to design several different tags, then fill the sheet with an assortment.

To print square tags, use a grid with 2 1/2-inch squares spaced out three across by four down on a letter-size layout.

Layout showing a variety of gift tag designs.

5. Print the layout on heavyweight matte photo paper, then cut out each tag. If you like, trim the top corners at 45° angles. Punch a hole in the top of each tag about 1/4 inch from the edge, either centered or at the corner.

6. (Opt.) Adhere Avery self-adhesive hole reinforcements to the front and back of the tag, or attach eyelets.

7. Fold a length of complementary ribbon, raffia, cord, or string in half, push the folded end through the hole, then thread the loose ends through the loop and pull them taut.

Slider Cards

When is a card more than a card? When it's a slider! A flat card glides into a custom sleeve and becomes . . . a slider. Sliders are fun for just about any occasion: the birth of a baby, an open house, Valentine's Day, birthdays, Easter, Halloween, or any holiday. The variations are endless: Add a collage, embellishment, or greeting to the sleeve, change the color of the eyelet, or add an eclectic assortment of fibers, a tassel, beads, and/or charms to the pull.

You Will Need

- Sturdy card stock (a letter-size sheet makes two sleeves)
- Bone folder—to score card stock
- Heavyweight matte photo paper*
- One or more photos
- Large circle punch
- Eyelets
- Hole punch, eyelet setter, and rubber mallet
- Paper cutter, scissors, or craft knife
- Ruler
- Self-healing cutting mat
- Complementary ribbon, fiber, raffia, cord, or string
- Beads or charms
- Scotch Quick-Dry Tacky Adhesive or double-sided tape
- Envelopes
  *For sturdier hanging ornament sliders, use Arches Infinity 355-gm White Textured photo paper.

TIP
If you're going to be incorporating a photo with a horizontal orientation (as in the Joy Peace Love slider shown in the photo), you may want to adapt the entire project to suit that orientation by laying out the insert and/or decorating the sleeve accordingly.

Make the Sleeve

When making the sleeve, choose a color of card stock that will complement the slider card.

1. Cut a piece of letter-size card stock in half vertically, then score and fold each half to form 4 1/4 x 5 1/2-inch sleeves.

2. Apply a thin line of craft glue or double-sided tape to the inside side edges of the top or bottom half of the folded card stock, then close the card and press firmly to adhere.

The slider insert can be used as a bookmark or hanging holiday decoration—a little gift in itself. (Fonts: Bernhard Modern, P22 Cezanne, and Gill Sans)

3. Use the circle punch to punch a half-circle "thumb" hole through both layers of card stock to aid in sliding the insert out. Place the sleeve under weight (e.g., some heavy books) so the glue sets and dries thoroughly.

Create the Slider Insert

Use the design concepts presented in Chapter 2 to lay out the insert.

1. In Photoshop, open a new file with a custom size of 2.125 x 5.5 inches (300 ppi, RGB). Lay out the slider insert design incorporating a photograph and text. Flatten the layers (Layer>Flatten Image).

2. To make multiple inserts at one time, open a new letter-size file in Photoshop (300 ppi). Drag out horizontal and vertical Guides to delineate eight equal segments as shown.

Set up a layout like this to create eight inserts.

3. Copy and paste or click and drag the insert layout into the new file eight times, moving each layout into position within the Guides. Make sure no part of the layout falls within the area outside the printable margins. Print and trim each layout to size.

4. Punch a hole at the center top of each insert. An eyelet adds a nice decorative touch, but it's optional.

5. Slip the loop of a folded length of ribbon or cord through the hole, threading the ends through the loop and pulling them taut.

A Few More Ideas

Have fun with this project by taking it a step further.

- Follow the instructions for the Film Strip Birth Announcement on page 120 to create a film-strip-style slider insert. Add a greeting in the last frame, print the layout on heavyweight matte paper, and fold it in half to fit.
- Use a sewing machine to stitch the edges of the sleeve together instead of using glue or double-sided tape. Trim the sides and top edge with decorative scissors.
- Use colored tape on the outside of the sleeve to seal the sides, adding a strip along the bottom to complete the look.
- Wrap the sleeve with a band of complementary handmade paper or decorate with collage. You may need to use a larger mailing envelope to accommodate this type of embellishment.

Slide Mount Ornaments

Film transparencies are often encased in slide mounts for protection and ease of storage and handling. Here they've been adapted to create hanging picture frame ornaments. Start a wonderful yearly tradition by making a different ornament to commemorate each year. Soon your friends and family will have an heirloom collection of unique, personalized ornaments. Vary the colors of the corner mounts and eyelets and use different cord and embellishments to personalize your design.

These fanciful hanging ornaments make a subtle allusion to the world of photography by adapting slide mounts as miniature frames.

You Will Need

- **35mm slide mounts (available at photo supply outlets in black or white and varying sizes)**
- **Marvy Liquid Gold opaque paint marker**
- **Photos**
- **Heavyweight matte photo paper**
- **Eyelets**
- **Craft punch, eyelet setter, and rubber mallet**
- **Gold photo corners**
- **Gold embroidery thread or cord**
- **Beads or charms (optional)**
- **Gold or silver card stock**
- **Craft glue**

1. For a delicate gilded effect, carefully run the tip of the marker along the inside and outside rims of the mount. The marker should be well primed.

2. If necessary, in Photoshop, resize photos to 1 x 1½ inches, then print on heavyweight matte photo paper.

3. Insert a trimmed photo in the slide mount and seal (many slide mounts are self-sealing; otherwise, use glue or double-sided tape).

4. Apply a small dab of glue to each corner and slip on photo corners, or use tape to hold them in place on the back of the mount.

5. Punch a hole at the top center of the slide mount and set the eyelet in the hole.

6. Slip the loop of a folded length of embroidery thread or cord through the hole and thread the ends through the loop, pulling them taut. Add beads or charms if desired.

7. Cut card stock into a 2 x 2-inch square and adhere it to the back of the ornament to finish.

A tiny book featuring slide mount "pages" containing miniature Auratones is further enhanced by handmade paper and gold eyelets, jump rings, photo corners, and ribbon.

A Few More Ideas

As with most of the projects in this book, this one is easily enhanced by your personal creative interpretation.

- Use black slide mounts with black-and-white or sepia-toned photos, or even Auratones (see 61).
- Add a handwritten note or caption on the front or back of each mount.
- Decorate the mount further with papers, collage, rubber stamps, or paints.
- Add eyelets along bottom of the mount and dangle beads, tiny ornaments, crystals, etc.

Family Photo Calendars

Even in this high-tech world, people still use and enjoy looking at printed calendars. Calendars are an excellent way to show off favorite images, and they lend themselves well to seasonal themes and color schemes. This design features a single photo and a yearly calendar and folds into a handy folio, but you can easily customize the design to include more photos or to create a new calendar for each month of the year.

You Will Need

- **Heavyweight matte photo paper**
- **Photo**
- **Decorative paper**
- **Paper cutter, scissors, or craft knife**
- **Ruler**
- **Self-healing cutting mat**
- **Spray adhesive (optional)**
- **Craft glue**
- **Waxed linen thread**
- **Needle**
- **Buttons or beads**

1. Create a 7 3/4 x 10-inch layout and insert a photo or multiple photos in the top half.

2. Download a free, printable calendar grid at www.bsmithphotography.com/goodies. Open the file in Photoshop, and unlock the layers by clicking on the lock icon for each layer in the Layers palette. Select all layers and, holding down the Shift key to center the layout, drag the calendar into your open file. Use the down arrow key to nudge it into position in the lower half of your layout. If necessary, go to Edit>Transform>Scale and drag the handles and/or adjust the percentages in the Options Bar until it fills the space properly.

   You can customize the calendar by using the Eraser tool (E) to erase existing text (make sure the Foreground color in the Toolbox is white) and replace it with typestyles to suit your fancy. You can even add important dates, and you might also want to use the Paint Bucket tool (G) or Paintbrush (B) to add color.

TIP

The folio calendar shown on page 159 incorporates the natural edges of the handmade paper for a rough-hewn look, and the cut edges were distressed a bit to enhance the look. If your paper has smooth edges, you can tear them to mimic the effect of mold-made edges.

Print and adhere a one-sheet calendar to decorative paper and make a folio. Here, two complementary papers were glued together back-to-back. Vintage buttons add an eclectic touch.

This calendar folds into a little folio for portability, but, honestly, it's just plain fun to wrap and unwrap.

NOTE

The 7 3/4-inch width means you can print on letter-size sheets, which will accommodate images that are large enough to be seen clearly and text large enough to be read easily, but if you have a printer that prints larger sheets, by all means take advantage of it.

3. Print and trim to size.

4. Cut a piece of heavyweight decorative paper to 7 7/8 × 17 inches. If you wish, you can fuse two sheets together back-to-back with spray adhesive.

5. Turn up the bottom 1 inch of the short side of the decorative paper and glue it to itself to create a finished edge. Fold down the top 1 inch of the paper, fold it over again, and glue it down for a sturdy finished edge.

6. Adhere the back of the calendar to the inside of the decorative paper so that just a tiny border shows along the side and bottom edges.

7. Fold the folio so that the calendar portion is folded in half and the top flap is folded over the top.

8. Thread a needle with a 30-inch length of waxed linen thread and, using a double strand of thread, attach a button to the outside of the flap. Add another button to the end of the thread and tie a knot to finish it off.

9. Close the folio and wrap the thread down and around the folio and once around the stationary button to secure.

Go to www.bsmithphotography.com/goodies and download the monthly calendar template. Then use what you've learned in this book to make them your own. Initially, it may take a fair amount of time, but you'll save countless hours in the future by working with templates and adapting them to the projects at hand.

Index